Understanding
Google Docs

2021 Edition

Kevin Wilson

www.elluminetpress.com

Understanding Google Docs: 2021 Ed

iStock.com/golibo, PeopleImages, ymgerman. Photo 130859010 © Kaspars Grinvalds - Dreamstime. com. Photo 103557713 © Konstantin Kolosov - Dreamstime.com. Yuri Arcurs via Getty Images, Cover Image by Chris Bardgett / Alamy Stock Photo, iStockPhoto elenabs

Publisher: Elluminet Press
Director: Kevin Wilson
Lead Editor: Steven Ashmore
Technical Reviewer: Mike Taylor, Robert Ashcroft
Copy Editors: Joanne Taylor, James Marsh
Proof Reader: Mike Taylor
Indexer: James Marsh
Cover Designer: Kevin Wilson

eBook versions and licenses are also available for most titles. Any source code or other supplementary materials referenced by the author in this text is available to readers at www.elluminetpress.com/resources

For detailed information about how to locate your book's resources, go to www.elluminetpress.com/resources

Table of Contents

About the Author...7

Acknowledgements..9

Introducing Google Docs...10

Getting Started...16
    Creating a Google Account......................................17
    Sign In..18
    Get Started 19
        Menus & Toolbars.. 20
        Page Rulers.. 21
    Download Google Chrome 22

Building Documents 24
    Creating a New Document 25
    Entering Text...26
    Dictate Text 26
        Setup.. 26
        Voice Commands 28
    Selecting Text 29
    Text Justification..30
    Paragraph Indents 31
        Indenting a Line... 31
        First Line Indent 31
        Hanging Indent.. 32
        Customize Indents with the Ruler...................... 34
        Tab Stops.. 35
    Paragraph Spacing..37
    Line Spacing..38
    Cut, Copy & Paste 39
        Cut & Paste... 39
        Copy & Paste 41
        Paste without Formatting.................................. 43
    Bold, Italic & Underlined..44
    Superscript & Subscript 45
    Highlighting Text 46
    Text Color..47

Text Size...47

Change Font...48

Change Case...49

Paragraph Styles..50

Bullet Lists 51

Numbered Lists 51

Inserting Symbols..52

Hidden Characters...53

Hyper-links..55

Equations...56

Page & Section Breaks 59

    Inserting Page Breaks.................................... 59

    Inserting Section Breaks................................ 60

Headers and Footers 61

    Inserting Headers 61

    Inserting Footers 62

    Formatting Headers and Footers.................. 63

Footnotes...65

Creating Columns..66

Contents Pages 67

Emojis 69

Adding Images & Graphics 70

Adding Images 71

    From Google Drive... 71

    Google Photos 72

    Upload from PC.. 73

    Web Search.. 74

    Camera on Laptop 76

    Camera on Tablet/Phone............................... 77

Resize Images 79

Rotate an Image...80

Cropping Images..81

Wrap Text around Images 83

Drawings..85

    WordArt 86

    Shapes 87

    Images 90

Tables and Charts 92

Tables...93

    Inserting Tables 93

    Text Formatting... 95

Cell Color 95
Borders 97
Cell Padding 99
Cell Alignment.. 100
Split Cells 101
Merge Cells 101
Row Height 102
Column Width... 102
Insert Row 103
Insert Column 105
Delete Column.. 106
Delete Row 106
Adding Charts 107
Customise your Chart.. 109
Chart Style 111
Chart & Axis Titles... 111
Data Series 112
Horizontal Axis 113
Vertical Axis.. 113
Gridlines and Ticks.. 114
Download & Publish Chart 115

Sharing and Collaboration.. **116**

Sharing a Document.. 117
Accepting the Invitation to Collaborate............................ 119
Editing Shared Documents 120
Making Edits... 120
Chatting with Other Collaborators............................. 120
Making Comments 121
Reply to Comment.. 122
Resolve a Comment 122
Making Suggestions.. 123
Sharing a Link.. 125
Sharing a Link with Anyone 125
Restricted Links... 127
People without Google Accounts..................................... 129
Stop Sharing a File 131
Smart Chips 132

Managing Documents... **134**

Opening Documents 135
Uploading Documents.. 137
Downloading & Converting Documents 139

Printing Documents 140
    Page Setup 140
    Print 143
Email as Attachment 147
Document Translation 149
Define & Lookup 150
Spelling & Grammar 151
Add-ons 154
    Install 154
    Manage Add-ons 157
    Useful Add-ons 157

Using Tablets **158**

Download Google Docs 159
Getting Started 160
Formatting Text 163
Paragraph Formatting 164
Insert Images 165
Resize Image 167
Insert Table 168
Insert Row 169
Insert Column 169
Format your Table 170

Using Google Drive **172**

Opening Google Drive 173
    On the Web 173
    The App 173
Getting Around Google Drive 174
Sync Files with your Computer 177
    Google Drive for Desktop 177
    Backup and Sync 177

Resources **182**

Video Resources 183
File Resources 185
Scanning the Codes 186
    iPhone 186
    Android 187

Index **188**

About the Author

With over 20 years' experience in the computer industry, Kevin Wilson has made a career out of technology and showing others how to use it. After earning a master's degree in computer science, software engineering, and multimedia systems, Kevin has held various positions in the IT industry including graphic & web design, digital film & photography, programming & software engineering, developing & managing corporate networks, building computer systems, and IT support.

He serves as senior writer and director at Elluminet Press Ltd, he periodically teaches computer science at college, and works as an IT trainer in England while researching for his PhD. His books have become a valuable resource among the students in England, South Africa, Canada, and in the United States.

Kevin's motto is clear: "If you can't explain something simply, then you haven't understood it well enough." To that end, he wrote the Exploring Tech Computing series, in which he breaks down complex technological subjects into smaller, easy-to-follow steps that students and ordinary computer users can put into practice.

Acknowledgements

Thanks to all the staff at Luminescent Media & Elluminet Press for their passion, dedication and hard work in the preparation and production of this book.

To all my friends and family for their continued support and encouragement in all my writing projects.

To all my colleagues, students and testers who took the time to test procedures and offer feedback on the book

Finally thanks to you the reader for choosing this book. I hope it helps you to use Google Docs with greater understanding.

1

Introduc-ing Google Docs

Google Docs was originally called Writely created by a company called Upstartle which Google acquired in 2006. After the acquisition, Writely was re-branded as Google Docs and became part of the Google Drive suite of productivity applications.

Google Docs is a free cloud-based word processor that allows you to create, edit, and share documents with ease. It is part of the Google Drive suite of productivity tools which also includes Google Sheets, Google Slides, and Google Forms.

Google Docs runs in a web browser on Windows and Mac platforms. There is also an app available for Android tablets and phones, as well as for iPhone or iPad.

One of the significant advantages of using Google Docs is the ability to collaborate in real-time. There are various collaborative features allowing teams and multiple users to work on projects together in real-time from locations all over the world.

To use Google Docs, you will need a Google Account. See "Creating a Google Account" on page 17 for more information.

Google Docs is a cloud based web application meaning it is hosted on a remote server and accessed over the internet through a web browser or light weight mobile app. Is available on multiple platforms such as MacOS, Windows 10/11, Linux and Chromebook, as well as on iPhone, iPad, Android tablets and phones.

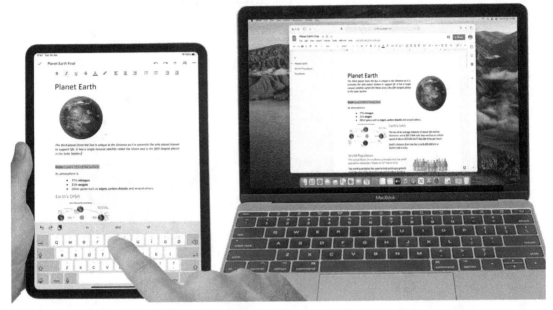

One of the main benefits of cloud-based applications is that they allow users to access their files from anywhere with an internet connection.

This is because the documents you create are saved onto Google Drive which is a cloud based storage service that allows you to access your files from anywhere and on any device. You get 15GB of free cloud storage - additional storage can be purchased if needed.

Also included are tools to convert documents to other formats such as Microsoft Word, Open Office, as well as PDF documents. This allows you to send these documents to other people who might be using other operating systems and software.

Chapter 1: Introducing Google Docs

Multiple users can open a document at the same time using Google Docs' collaboration features. These other users can be anywhere in the world with an internet connection.

Here, you can see two other people editing a document in real time. The edits other users are working on are indicated with their name tag.

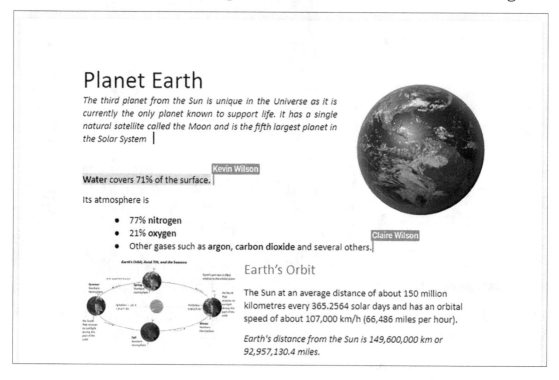

Google Docs allows you to translate a document into another language, which can be a useful feature if you're dealing with international correspondence. The translations, however, are not perfect and sometimes you'll find errors or sentences that have not translated correctly. Here's my document translated from English into Spanish

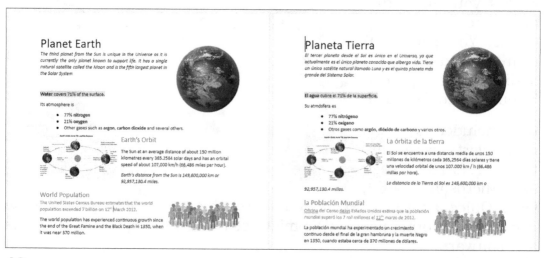

You'll find tools to check spelling and grammar as you type.

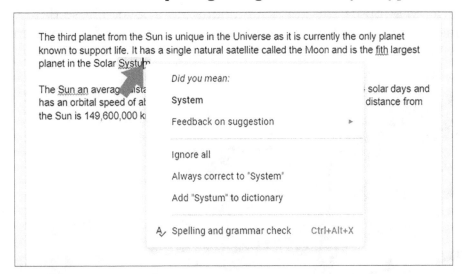

You can also expand Google Doc's functionality with addons. These add ons are developed mostly by third party developers.

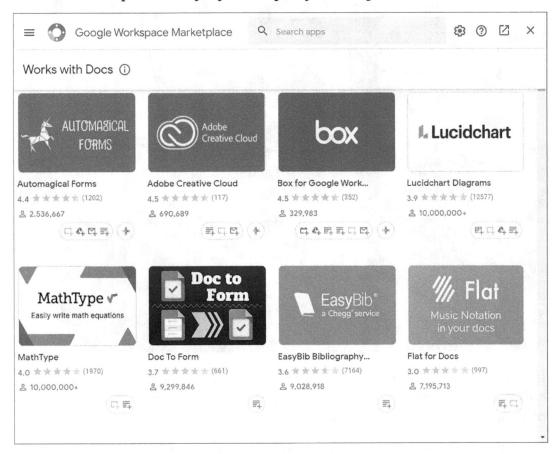

You'll find addons for mail merge, spelling, grammar and translators. As well as diagramming tools, equation editors and mathematical tools.

Chapter 1: Introducing Google Docs

Google operates multiple data centers and server farms located around the world to support the services discussed above. These data centers are massive facilities that house tens of thousands of servers and data storage devices.

In the photograph above, there are over 20 servers stacked up in each cabinet and hundreds of cabinets filling entire rooms serving millions of people who subscribe to the service.

The advantage is, you can log in and access your files anywhere on the internet and your files are backed up by the cloud service, so should your computer fail, your files will still be on your Google Drive.

Google Drive is accessible using a web browser, all you have to do is navigate to the website and sign in with your Google Account email address and password.

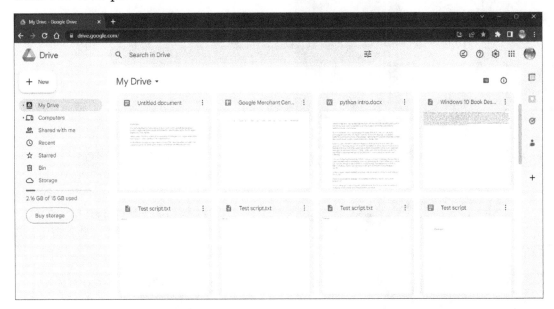

You can also download the app version which is available for iPhone/iPad and Android devices. Just search the relevant app store.

2

Getting Started

In this chapter we'll take a look at getting started with Google Docs using a web browser such as Google Chrome. You can also use Microsoft Edge if you're on a PC or Safari if you're on a Mac.

- Creating a Google Account

- How to Sign In

- Tour of the main screen

- Menus

- Toolbars

- Page Rulers

- Download Google Chrome

Have a look at the video resources section. Open your web browser and navigate to the following website.

e l l u m i n e t p r e s s . c o m / starting-googledocs

Creating a Google Account

If you use Gmail you will already have a Google Account. If this is the case, you don't need to create a new Google Account so you can skip this step.

If you don't have an account, you can create one online before you start. To do this, open your web browser and browse to the following page.

`accounts.google.com/signup`

Fill in your name in the first two fields, then under 'username', type in the name you want to appear in your email address. This can be a nickname or your full name. The name must be unique, so if someone else has already taken the name, you'll need to choose a new one or add a couple of numbers. Google will tell you if the username you entered has already been used.

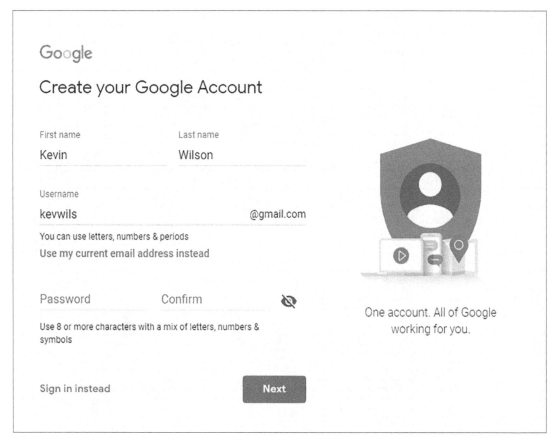

Enter the password you want to use in the 'password' field, then type it again to confirm it in the 'confirm' field.

Click 'next'.

Sign In

Once you have your Google Account, you can sign in. Google docs will run in any web browser, however Google recommend using their own Chrome browser. To start Google Docs, go to the following website:

`docs.google.com`

Sign in with your Google Account email address and password.

Once you sign in, you'll land on the Google Docs start or home screen.

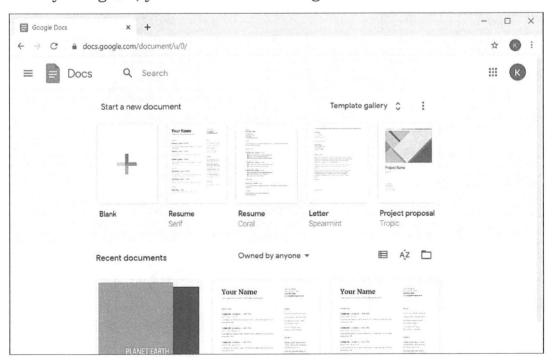

Get Started

Let's take a closer look at the start screen.

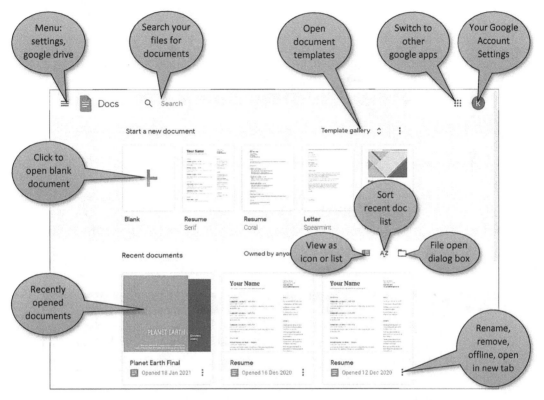

From here, you can create a new document. You can do this by selecting a blank document.

You can select a template from the pre-designed documents if you want to create a letter, report, or resume/cv. To do this click 'template gallery', then click on a template.

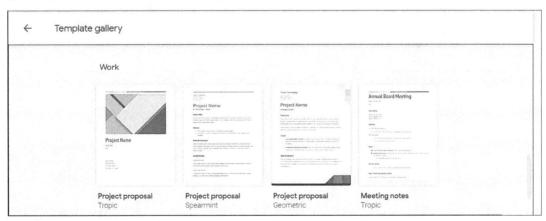

In this example, we're going to start a document from scratch, so select 'blank'

Menus & Toolbars

When you open a new document, you'll see a menu along the top of the screen

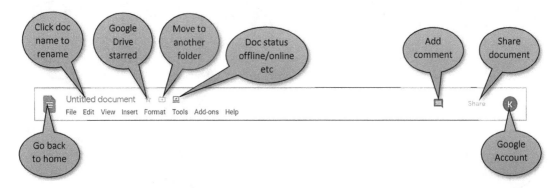

Under the document title there are pull-down menus. You will find various commands here for dealing with files, editing your document, as well as inserting tables, images, tools for grammar and spelling and so on.

Menu	Commands
File	Share document, create new document, open, make a copy. Email, download a copy, offline. Move, rename, publish on web, page setup, print.
Edit	Copy, paste, cut. Find, replace, select all.
View	Show ruler, view mode. Ruler, doc outline, equation, section breaks, full screen.
Insert	Image, table, drawing, chart, line, footnote. Special characters, equations. Headers, footers, link, comment. Table of contents
Format	Text, paragraph styles, alignment, indents, line spacing. Columns, bullets, numbering. Headers & footers, page numbers, page orientation, format image, format table.
Tools	Spelling, grammar, word count, review suggested edits, citations, dictionary, voice typing, preferences.

Underneath the menus along the top, you'll see a toolbar. This is where you'll find your formatting tools, font colours and sizes.

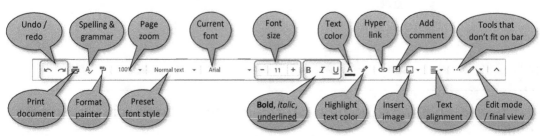

Page Rulers

The page ruler runs across the top of your page and is useful for setting your margins, paragraph indentations, and tab stops.

On the top left, you'll see three markers. The small rectangular one at the top is your first line indent - this indents the first line of the selected text. The small triangular one is the left indent - this indents all the selected text. The last marker is hidden by the other two, but if you move the markers out the way, you'll see the point where the ruler turns from white to grey. This is the left margin.

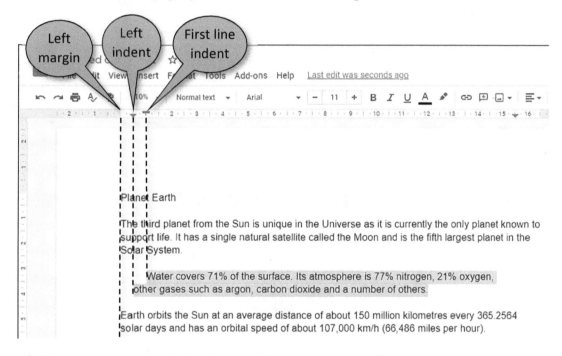

It's the same on the right hand side, you have a right indent and a right margin, but no first line indent.

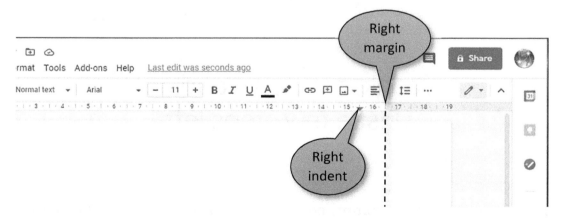

There is also a ruler that runs down the left hand side.

Download Google Chrome

Google Chrome is a fast and streamlined browser that is a good alternative to Microsoft Edge. To use Google Chrome, you'll first need to download it.

Open your current web browser and navigate to the following website. You can download Google Chrome from here.

```
www.google.com/chrome
```

Click the blue 'download chrome' button on the web page.

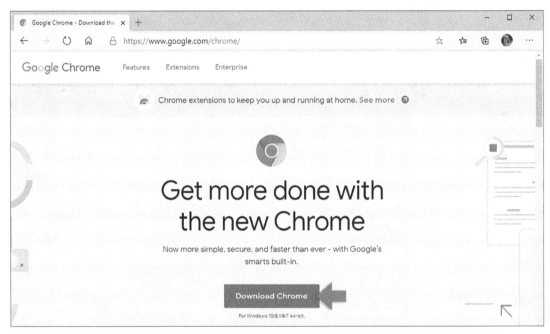

Click 'open' when prompted by your browser then follow the on screen instructions to install Chrome.

If you don't see the prompt, go to your downloads folder and double click 'chromesetup.exe'.

You'll find Chrome on your start menu and on your desktop. Click the chrome icon to start.

Once you open Chrome, sign in with your Google Account email address and password. Click the profile icon on the top right. Then click 'turn on sync.

Enter your Google Account email address and password when prompted. Click 'next'.

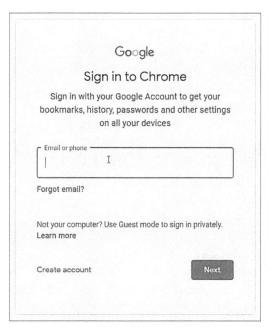
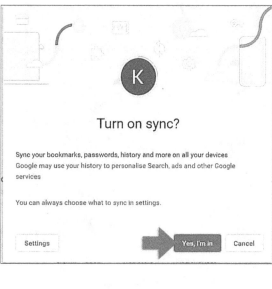

Click 'yes I'm in' to synchronise your data across all your devices. This is useful if you use your account on your iPad, phone, chromebook as well as on windows 10 or mac.

3 Building Documents

In this section, we're going to take a look at how to build a document using the various tools and features offered by Google Docs.

We'll go through creating a new document, entering or dictating text, as well as formatting text.

- Creating a New Document
- Entering Text
- Text Justification
- Paragraph Indents & Spacing
- Line Spacing
- Cut, Copy & Paste
- Bold, Italic, Underlined, Superscript & Subscript
- Text Color, and Size
- Paragraph Styles
- Bullet & Numbered Lists
- Equations
- Page & Section Breaks
- Headers & Footers
- Footnotes
- Creating Columns
- Contents Pages

Have a look at the video resources section. Open your web browser and navigate to the following website.

elluminetpress.com/ building-googledocs

Creating a New Document

To create a new document, select 'blank' from the Google Docs home page.

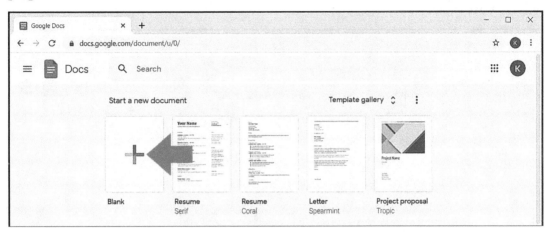

To get to the home page, click the 'docs' icon on the top left, or navigate to the following website:

`docs.google.com`

You can also select a template from the template gallery, if you want to write a letter or a report. To do this, click 'template gallery', then select a template.

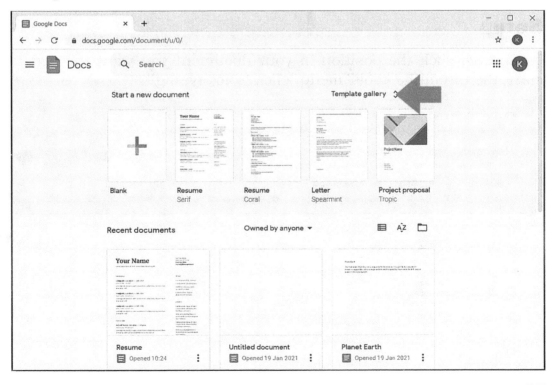

Entering Text

Use your keyboard to type in your text. You'll see a small flashing bar called a cursor (shown below). This tells you were the text will appear when you type.

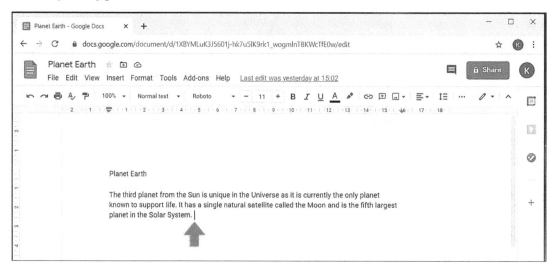

Dictate Text

If typing isn't your thing, you can dictate your text using the voice typing feature.

Setup

To do this, click the position in your document you want the text to start, then from the 'tools' menu, click 'voice typing'.

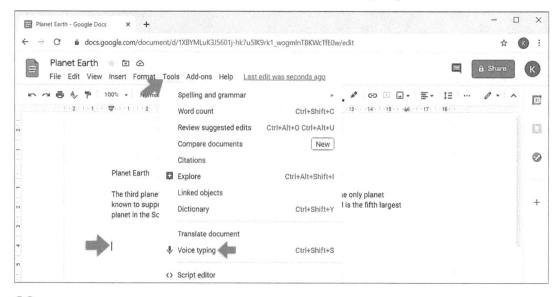

You'll see a mic icon appear on the left hand side of your screen. Click the icon to start.

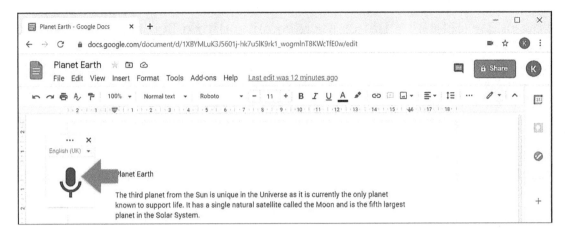

If you see a security prompt asking to use your microphone, click 'allow'.

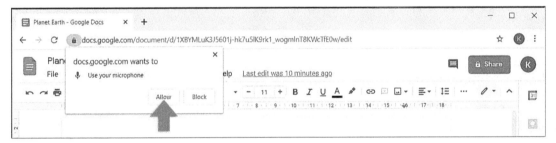

Now, you can dictate your text using your microphone.

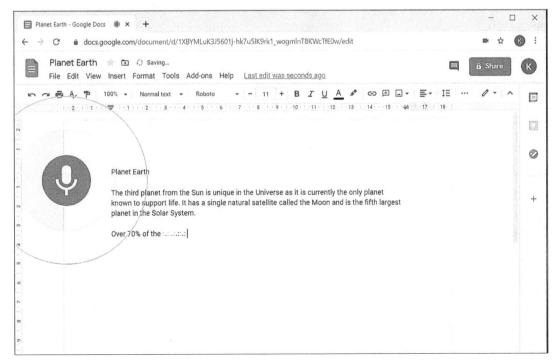

Voice Commands

Use the following phrases to add punctuation to your text. Make sure you pause before and after each command to differentiate it from an actual word.

```
Comma
Period
New line
New paragraph
Question mark
Exclamation point
```

To format your text use the following commands.

```
Bold
Italic
Subscript
Superscript
Underline
All caps
Decrease font size
Increase font size
Font size [6-400]
Create bulleted list
Create numbered list
```

To align your text use

```
Align center
Align justified
Align left
Align right
```

To select a word or paragraph use

```
Select all
Select line
Select paragraph
Select word
Unselect
Select none
Delete last word
Delete sentence
Go to start of line
Go to next paragraph
```

Selecting Text

To select text, click and drag your mouse over the text you want to select. The selected text with be highlighted in grey.

Planet Earth

The third planet from the Sun is unique in the Universe as it is currently the only planet known to support life. It has a single natural satellite called the Moon and is the fifth largest planet in the Solar System.

Water covers 71% of the surface. Its atmosphere is 77% nitrogen, 21% oxygen, other gases such as argon, carbon dioxide and a number of others.

Earth orbits the Sun at an average distance of about 150 million kilometres every 365.2564 solar days and has an orbital speed of about 107,000 km/h (66,486 miles per hour).

To quickly select a paragraph, triple click on any word in the paragraph.

Planet Earth

The third planet from the Sun is unique in the Universe as it is currently the only planet known to supp   It has a single natural satellite called the Moon and is the fifth largest planet in the So ar   em.

Water covers 71% of the surface. Its atmosphere is 77% nitrogen, 21% oxygen, other gases such as argon, carbon dioxide and a number of others.

Earth orbits the Sun at an average distance of about 150 million kilometres every 365.2564 solar days and has an orbital speed of about 107,000 km/h (66,486 miles per hour).

To quickly select a word, double click on it.

Planet Earth

The third planet from the Sun is unique in the Universe as it is currently the only planet known to support life. It has a single natural satellite called the Moon and is the fifth largest planet in the Solar System.

Water covers 71% of the surface. Its atmosphere is 77% nitrogen, 21% oxygen, other gases such as argon, carbon dioxide and a numbe   thers.

Earth orbits the Sun at an average distance of about 150 million kilometres every 365.2564 solar days and has an orbital speed of about 107,000 km/h (66,486 miles per hour).

Text Justification

You can justify your text to align it to the left or right margins. You can fully justify your text, meaning it is aligned with the left and right margins.

> The third planet from the Sun is unique in the Universe as it is currently the only planet known to support life. It has a single natural satellite called the Moon and is the fifth largest planet in the Solar System.

You can align the text to the right margin...

> Water covers 71% of the surface. Its atmosphere is 77% nitrogen, 21% oxygen, other gases such as argon, carbon dioxide and a number of others.

...you can align text to the centre of the page...

> Earth orbits the Sun at an average distance of about 150 million kilometres every 365.2564 solar days and has an orbital speed of about 107,000 km/h (66,486 miles per hour).

...or to the left margin.

> The United States Census Bureau estimates that the world population exceeded 7 billion on 12th March 2012. The world population has experienced continuous growth since the end of the Great Famine and the Black Death in 1350, when it was near 370 million.

To align text, first select it with your mouse, then click the alignment icon on the toolbar.

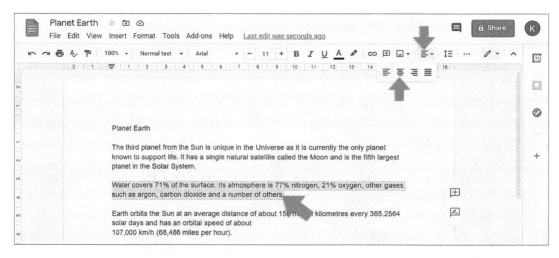

Select an alignment (left, centre, right, full justification).

Paragraph Indents

To increase the indent of a paragraph, select the text with your mouse so it's highlighted.

Indenting a Line

You can indent lines, paragraphs or lists to help separate them from the rest of your document. This can make documents easier to read. To indent text, select it with your mouse, then select the increase indent icon from the toolbar. *If the icon isn't there, click the three dots icon.*

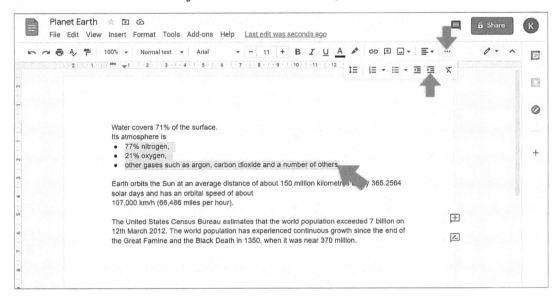

To decrease the indent, just select the decrease indent icon on the toolbar.

First Line Indent

The first line indent is a good way to begin paragraphs. This helps the reader to process the information and to identify sections in your text.

First select the text you want to indent, highlighting it with your mouse as shown below.

Planet Earth

The third planet from the Sun is unique in the Universe as it is currently the only planet known to support life. It has a single natural satellite called the Moon and is the fifth largest planet in the Solar System.

From the 'format' menu, select 'align and indent'. Click 'indentation options' on the slideout menu.

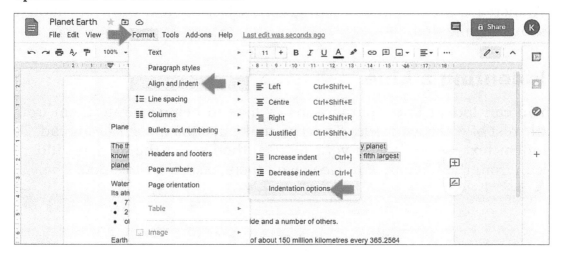

Under 'special indent' and select 'first line'. Set distance if required.

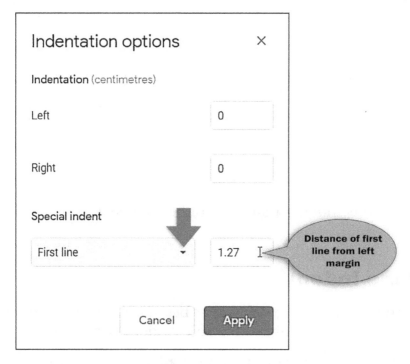

Hanging Indent

A hanging indent, indents all the lines except the first one. These indents are usually used with lists, bullet points or bibliographies.

Wilson. K (2016, March 4). Using Microsoft Office 2016: *Getting Started With Word, p34, Chapter 4.* Retrieved from   http://www.elluminetpress.com

First select the text you want to indent, highlighting it with your mouse as shown below.

Planet Earth

The third planet from the Sun is unique in the Universe as it is currently the only planet known to support life. It has a single natural satellite called the Moon and is the fifth largest planet in the Solar System.

From the 'format' menu, select 'align and indent'. Click 'indentation options' on the slideout menu.

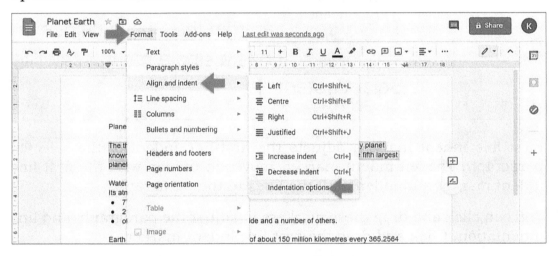

Under 'special indent', select 'hanging'. Set distance if required.

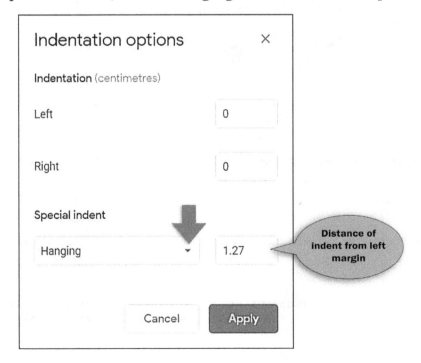

Customize Indents with the Ruler

If you look closely at the ruler. On the left hand side, you'll see two markers.

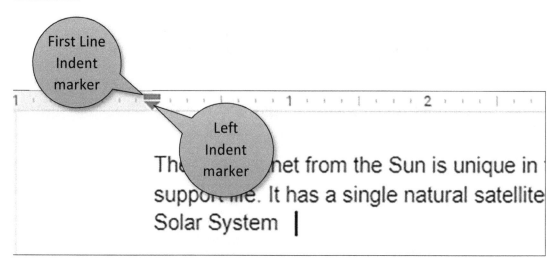

First line indent marker, adjusts the first-line indent of the selected paragraph. The left indent marker, moves in unison with the first line indent marker and indents all the lines in the paragraph.

You can click and drag these markers to adjust the paragraph and line indentation. Click and drag the first line indent marker.

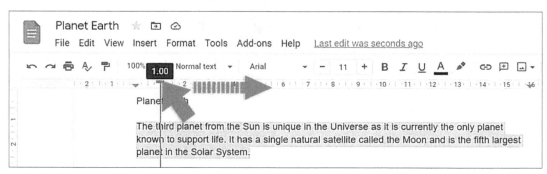

Once you release your mouse, the first line will indent.

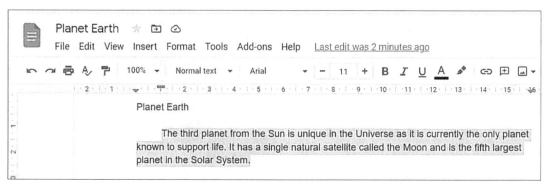

You can also indent the right hand side. To do this, drag the right indent marker as shown below.

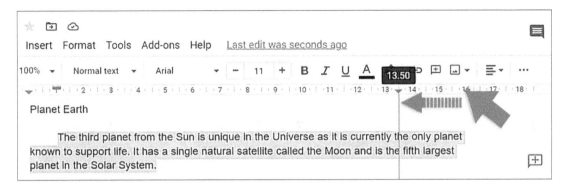

Tab Stops

Tab stops give you more control over the placement of your text. This allows you to tab out your text using the tab key on your keyboard. For example, tab out the following information.

> Water covers 71% of the surface. Its atmosphere is
>
> 77% nitrogen,
> 21% oxygen,
> 2% other gases such as argon and carbon dioxide.

To add a tab stop, select the text you want to tab. Right-click the location for the tab stop on the ruler along the top of your document. Eg 3cm.

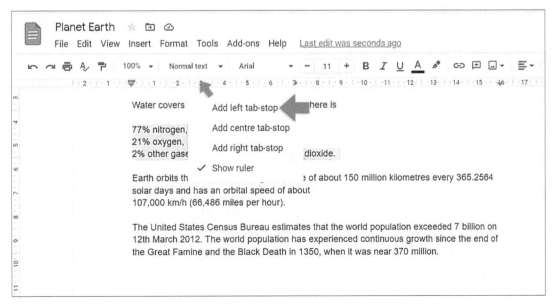

Select 'add left tab stop'.

Chapter 3: Building Documents

Now you can space out the data using the tab key. For example, if I want to tab the first line, eg separate "77%" and "nitrogen", click between the two and press the tab key on your keyboard.

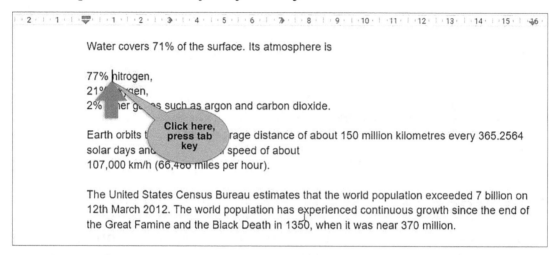

Do the same for the rest...

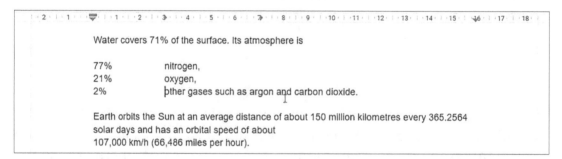

To remove a tab stop, just click on the marker on the ruler and drag it downwards.

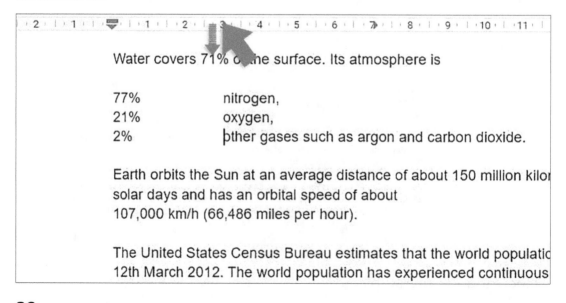

Paragraph Spacing

You can add space before and after a paragraph to help separate your paragraphs on the page.

> Space before paragraph
>
> The third planet from the Sun is unique in the Universe as it is currently the only planet known to support life. It has a single natural satellite called the Moon and is the fifth largest planet in the Solar System.
>
> Space after paragraph

To adjust the spacing, select the paragraph or paragraphs you want to adjust. From the 'format' menu, select 'line & paragraph spacing'. Click 'add space after paragraph'. *To add a custom spacing - select 'custom spacing' from the slideout... then enter the spacing in the 'paragraph spacing' section of the dialog box that appears.*

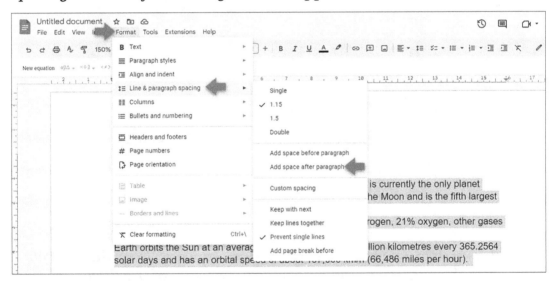

You'll see a space after each paragraph.

> The third planet from the Sun is unique in the Universe as it is currently the only planet known to support life. It has a single natural satellite called the Moon and is the fifth largest planet in the Solar System.
>
> Water covers 71% of the surface. Its atmosphere is 77% nitrogen, 21% oxygen, other gases such as argon, carbon dioxide and a number of others.
>
> Earth orbits the Sun at an average distance of about 150 million kilometres every 365.2564 solar days and has an orbital speed of about 107,000 km/h (66,486 miles per hour).
>
> The United States Census Bureau estimates that the world population exceeded 7 billion on 12th March 2012. The world population has experienced continuous growth since the end of the Great Famine and the Black Death in 1350, when it was near 370 million.

Line Spacing

Line spacing, as its name suggests, adjusts the spacing between the lines of text on your page.

> The third planet from the Sun is unique in the Universe as it is currently the only planet
>
> known to support life. It has a single natural satellite called the Moon and is the fifth largest
>
> planet in the Solar System.

First, select the text you want to adjust, then from the 'format' menu, select 'line & paragraph spacing'. Click one of the options circled below.

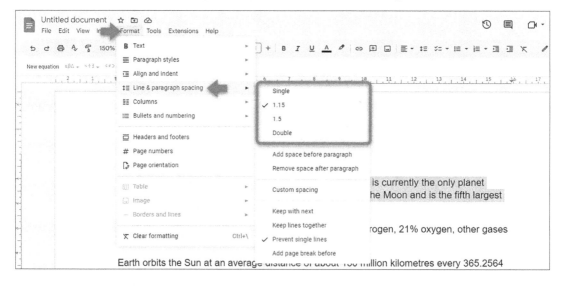

To add a custom spacing - select 'custom spacing' from the slideout... then enter the spacing in the 'line spacing' section of the dialog box that appears.

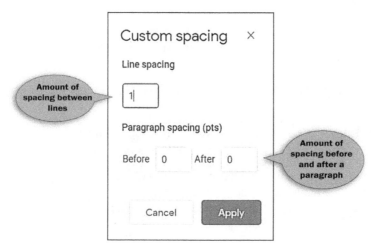

Cut, Copy & Paste

To ease editing documents, you can use copy, cut and paste to move paragraphs or pictures around on different parts of your document.

'Cut' moves the selected text from its original location, while 'copy' creates a duplicate of the selected text and leaving the original text in place.

Cut & Paste

First select the paragraph below with your mouse. To do this click before the word 'Earth', then drag your mouse across the line towards the end, as shown below.

> The third planet from the Sun is unique in the Universe as it is currently the only planet known to support life. It has a single natural satellite called the Moon and is the fifth largest planet in the Solar System. Earth's distance from the sun is 149,600,000 km.
>
> Click & drag across text to highlight

Once you have done that, select the 'edit' menu. From the drop down, click on 'cut'.

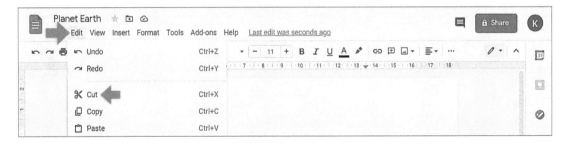

Now click on the position in the document you want the paragraph you just cut out to be inserted.

> Earth orbits the Sun at an average distance of about 150 million kilometres every 365.2564 solar days and has an orbital speed of about 107,000 km/h (66,486 miles per hour). |
>
> The United States Census Bureau estimates that the world population exceeded 7 billion on 12th March 2012. The world population has experienced continuous growth since the end of the Great Famine and the Black Death in 1350, when it was near 370 million.

Chapter 3: Building Documents

Once you have done that, go back to the 'edit' menu and select 'paste'.

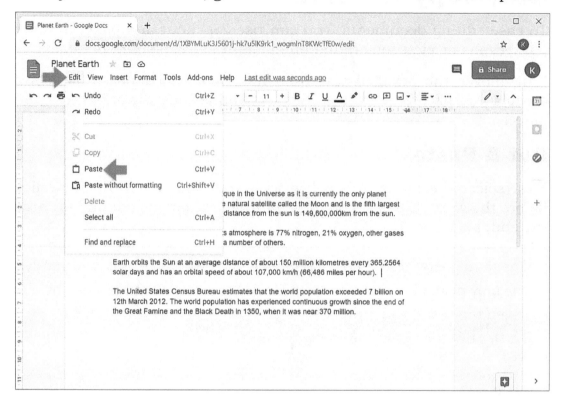

Here, we can see the sentence we cut out earlier has been pasted into position

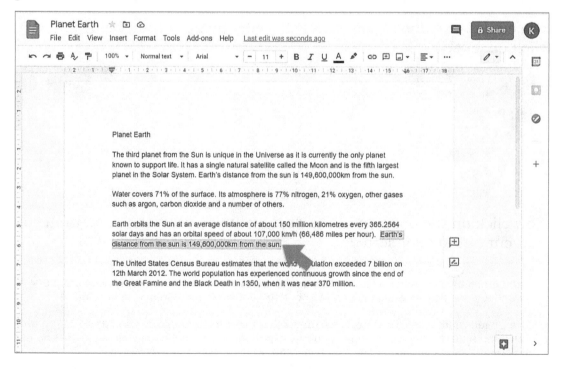

Copy & Paste

If you wanted to copy something ie make a duplicate of the text, then use the same procedure except click 'copy' instead of 'cut'.

First select the paragraph below with your mouse. To do this click before the word 'Earth', then drag your mouse across the line towards the end, as shown below.

> The third planet from the Sun is unique in the Universe as it is currently the only planet known to support life. It has a single natural satellite called the Moon and is the fifth largest planet in the Solar System. Earth's distance from the sun is 149,600,000 km.
>
> Click & drag across text to highlight

Once you have done that, select the 'edit' menu. From the drop down, click on 'cut'.

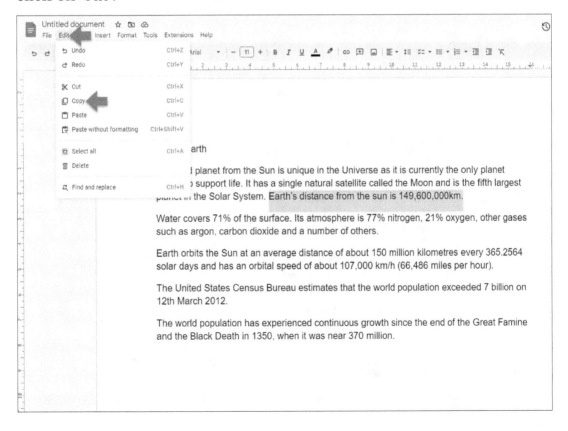

Chapter 3: Building Documents

Now click on the position in the document you want the paragraph you just cut out to be inserted.

> The third planet from the Sun is unique in the Universe as it is currently the only planet known to support life. It has a single natural satellite called the Moon and is the fifth largest planet in the Solar System.
>
> Water covers 71% of the surface. Its atmosphere is 77% nitrogen, 21% oxygen, other gases such as argon, carbon dioxide and a number of others.
>
> Earth orbits the Sun at an average distance of about 150 million kilometres every 365.2564 solar days and has an orbital speed of about 107,000 km/h (66,486 miles per hour). |
>
> The United States Census Bureau estimates that the world population exceeded 7 billion on 12th March 2012. The world population has experienced continuous growth since the end of the Great Famine and the Black Death in 1350, when it was near 370 million.

Once you have done that, go back to the 'edit' menu and select 'paste'.

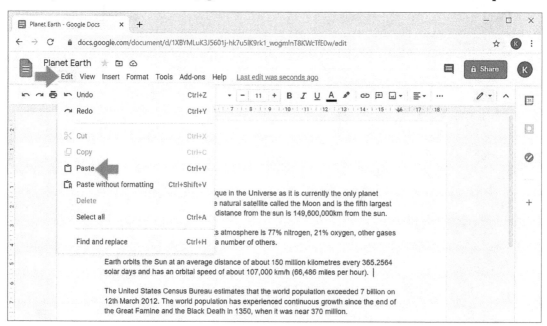

Here, you can see that we've copied the text.

> The third planet from the Sun is unique in the Universe as it is currently the only planet known to support life. It has a single natural satellite called the Moon and is the fifth largest planet in the Solar System. Earth's distance from the sun is 149,600,000km.
>
> Water covers 71% of the surface. Its atmosphere is 77% nitrogen, 21% oxygen, other gases such as argon, carbon dioxide and a number of others.
>
> Earth orbits the Sun at an average distance of about 150 million kilometres every 365.2564 solar days and has an orbital speed of about 107,000 km/h (66,486 miles per hour). Earth's distance from the sun is 149,600,000km.
>
> The United States Census Bureau estimates that the world population exceeded 7 billion on 12th March 2012.

Paste without Formatting

Paste without formatting is a command that is used to paste text without carrying over any formatting from the source text. This is useful when you want to paste text without altering the formatting of the document you are pasting into.

For example, when you copy text from a web page, another document, or any source that contains formatting information, that formatting information is also copied along with the text. This means that when you paste the text into a new location, it retains the formatting from the source.

The formatting is usually different to what you've got in your Google Docs page. You can use 'paste without formatting' to paste in the text with no original formatting so it will match the formatting in your document.

If we copy the text from the web page shown below, we just want the text, not the font, text size, or text color. Highlight the text on the webpage, then press control C on your keyboard to copy.

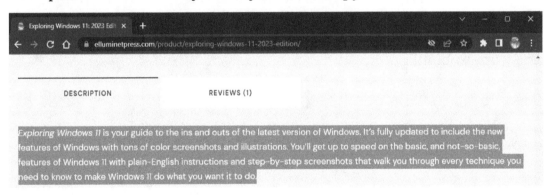

To paste this into our document, go up to the edit menu, then select 'paste without formatting'.

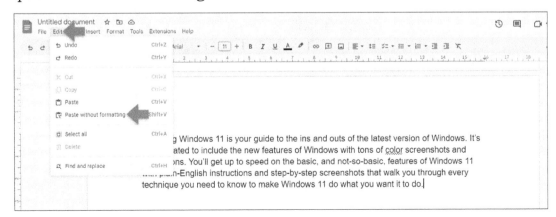

Bold, Italic & Underlined

You can use **bold**, *italic* or <u>underlined</u> text to emphasise certain words or paragraphs.

To do this, select the text you want to apply formatting to, then from the toolbar along the top of the screen, select one of the icons: **bold**, *italic* or <u>underlined</u>.

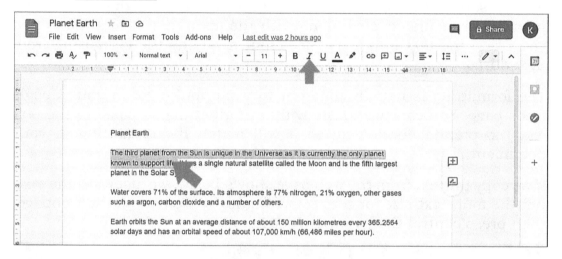

To make the text "water", "nitrogen" and "oxygen" bold, double click on the word to highlight it.

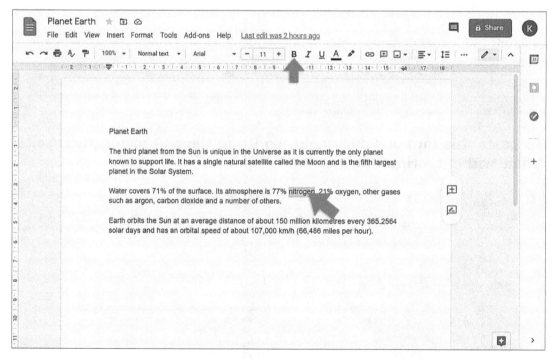

Select the bold icon from the toolbar.

Superscript & Subscript

Subscripts appear below the text line, and are used primarily in mathematical formulas to express chemical compounds or footnotes.

For example.

H_2O or CO_2

You can add subscripts to your text. To do this, first highlight the character you want to make into a subscript. In this example, I want to select the '2' in H20. From the 'format menu' select 'text', then click 'subscript' on the slideout menu.

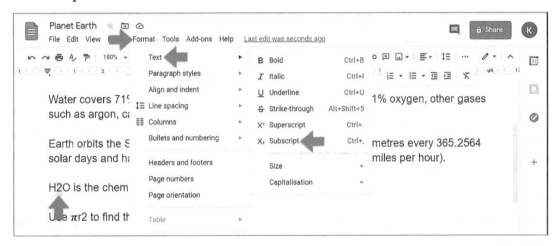

Superscripts appear at the top of the text line and are used primarily in mathematical formulas, such as the area of the circle is = πr^2

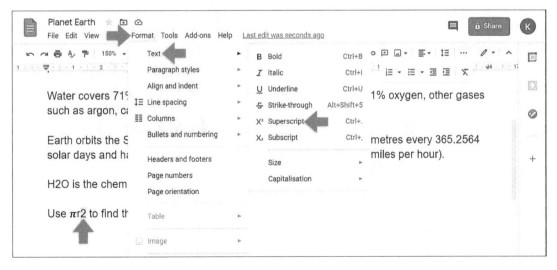

Select the '2' from the formula $\pi r2$. From the 'format menu' select 'text', then click 'subscript' from the slideout menu.

Highlighting Text

You can highlight words, sentences and paragraphs to make important information stand out. To do this, first select the text with your mouse.

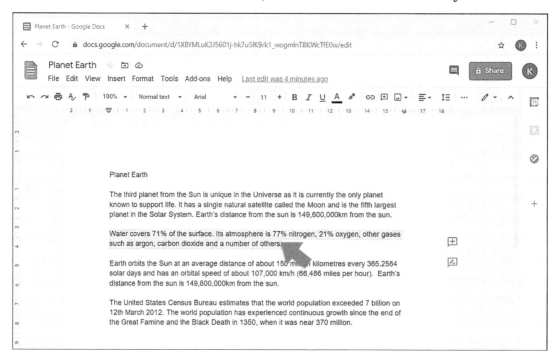

Click the highlight icon on the toolbar, then select a color from the palette.

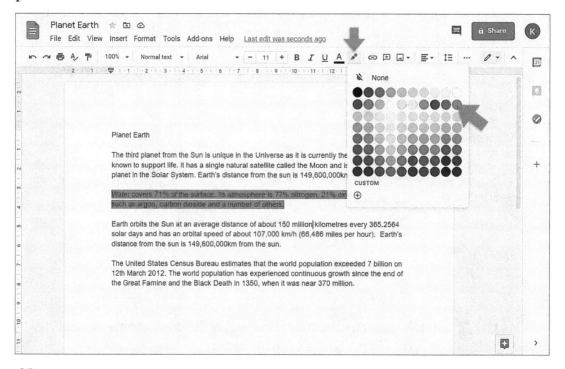

Text Color

To change the color of the text, first highlight it with your mouse. In the example below, I want to change the text color of the first paragraph. To do this, click before the word 'the' and drag your mouse across the paragraph, to the end after 'March 2012', to highlight it.

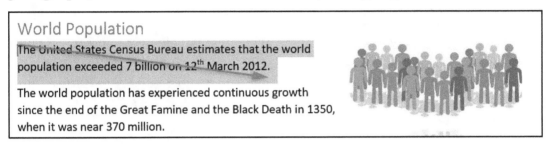

Click the text color icon on the toolbar, then select a color from the palette.

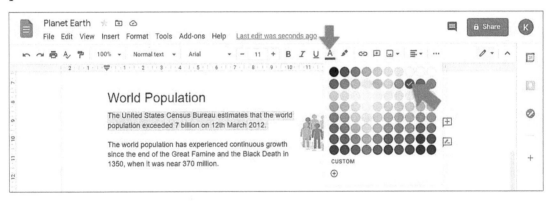

Text Size

To change the size of the text, select it with your mouse, then use the font size controls on the toolbar.

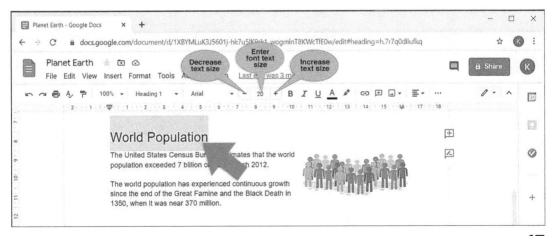

Change Font

To change the font, select it the text with your mouse.

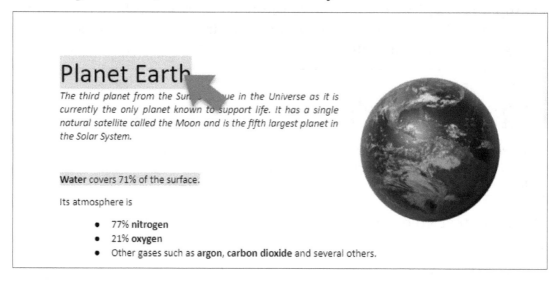

From the toolbar, click on the typeface drop down menu, then select a font from the list.

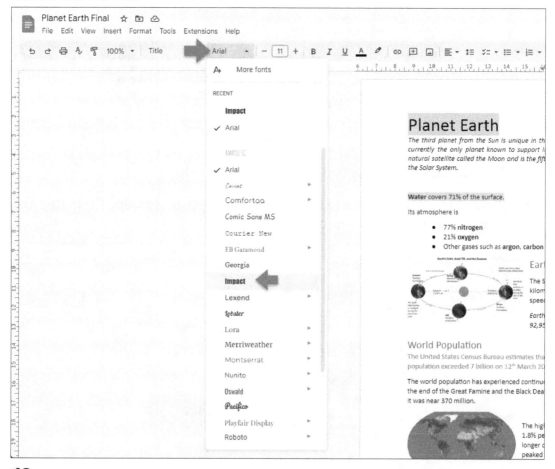

Change Case

You can change the case of a word or sentence using the change case feature. You can use:

lowercase text

UPPERCASE TEXT

Title Case, Capitalises First Letter Of Each Word

To change the case of a word or sentence, first highlight it with your mouse.

Planet earth

The third planet from the Sun is unique in the Universe as it is currently the only planet known to support life. It has a single natural satellite called the Moon and is the fifth largest planet in the Solar System.

Water covers 71% of the surface. Its atmosphere is 77% nitrogen, 21% oxygen, other gases such as argon, carbon dioxide and a number of others.

Earth orbits the Sun at an average distance of about 150 million kilometres every 365.2564 solar days and has an orbital speed of about 107,000 km/h (66,486 miles per hour).

From the 'format' menu, go down to 'text', select 'capitalisations' from the slideout menu.

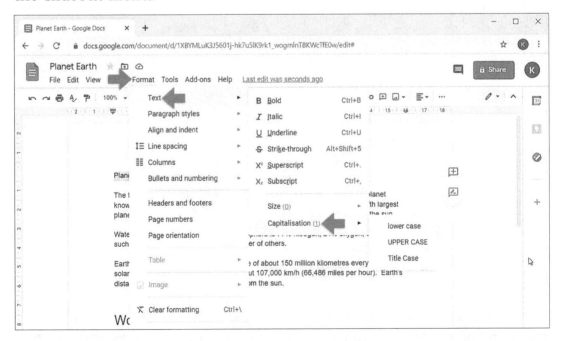

Select either 'lower case', 'UPPER CASE' or 'Title Case'.

Paragraph Styles

Docs has numerous paragraph styles that are useful for keeping your formatting consistent. The idea is to format all your headings with 'title', 'heading 1', 'heading 2', 'heading 3', your main text as 'normal', and so on. This makes it easier to format your document so you don't have to apply the same font style, size and color manually every time you want a heading.

To apply the styles to a heading or paragraph, highlight it with your mouse as shown below.

The third planet from the Sun is unique in the Universe as it is currently the only planet known to support life. It has a single natural satellite called the Moon and is the fifth largest planet in the Solar System.

Select a style from the styles drop down box on the toolbar.

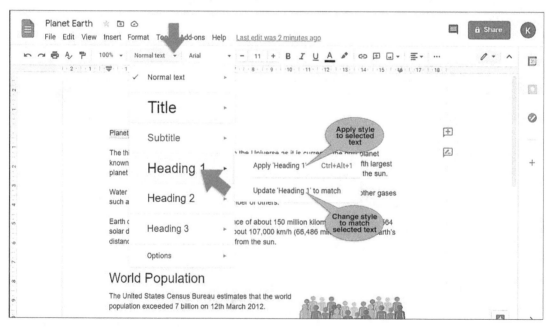

Click on a style to apply it to the selected text. Click the small to the right and select 'update to match' if you want to assign the current text formatting to the style.

Bullet Lists

We can edit the document and change the sentence explaining atmospheric composition to a bullet point list. First, select the text using your mouse as shown below.

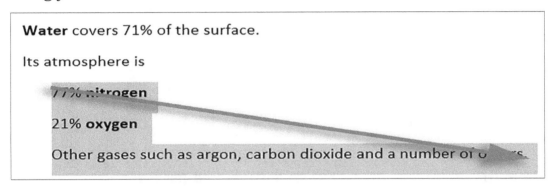

From the toolbar click the small down arrow next to the bullet list icon. If the icon isn't there, click the three dots icon on the right hand side of the toolbar.

From the drop down menu, select a bullet style.

Numbered Lists

We can edit the document and change the sentence explaining atmospheric composition to a numbered point list. Select the text using your mouse as shown below.

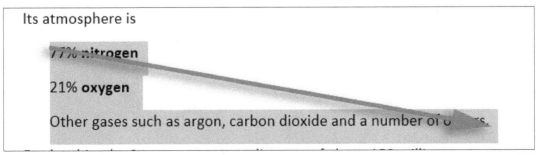

From the toolbar click the small down arrow next to the numbered list icon. If the icon isn't there, click the three dots icon on the right hand side of the toolbar.

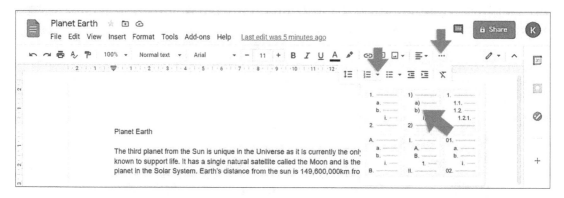

From the drop down menu, select a numbered list style.

Inserting Symbols

You can insert special symbols for mathematics, emojis, and special punctuation characters.

In the example sentence below, I want to insert the degree symbol after the number 40.

Last summer we saw temperatures of up to 40|

To insert a symbol, go to the 'insert' menu then select 'special character'.

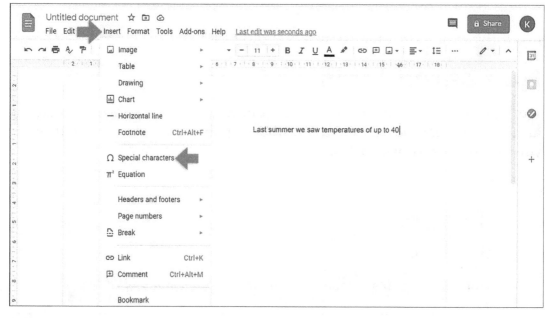

Select the character from the dialog box. If you can't find it, try searching for it using the search field on the right hand side.

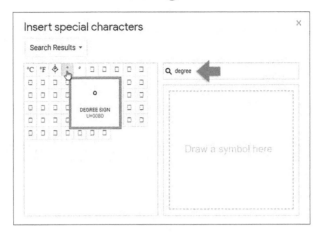

Click on the one you want to add.

Last summer we saw temperatures of up to 40°|

Hidden Characters

Google Docs inserts formatting characters such as carriage returns, spaces, tab characters that are hidden by default, to make editing your document easier for you.

To see these characters, you'll first need to install an add-on. Go to the 'add-ons' menu, then select 'get add-ons'. Type show into the search field.

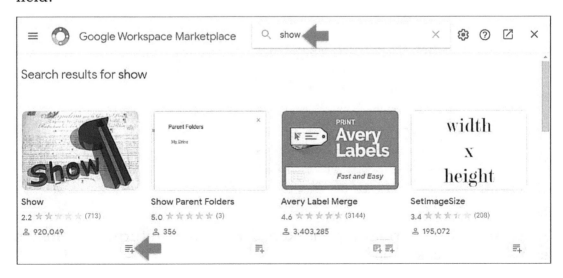

Click the small 'add' icon underneath the add-on's thumbnail icon.

Click the 'install' button. You may be prompted to enter your Google Account email address and password.

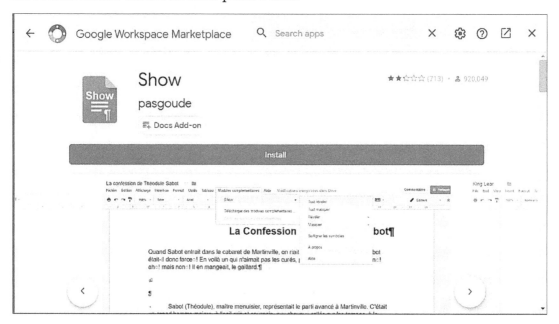

Once the add-on is installed, go to the 'add-ons' menu, go down to 'show', then select 'show all' from the slideout menu.

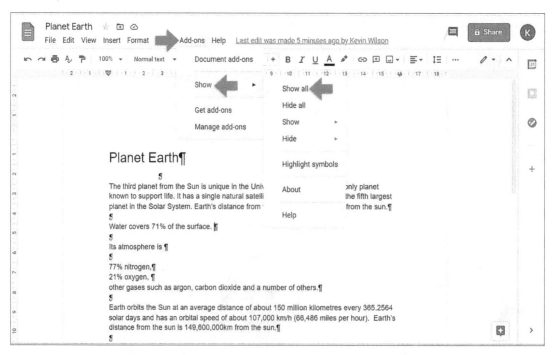

You'll see all the formatting markers for carriage return, line breaks and section breaks appear.

To remove the formatting markers, just select 'hide all' from the menu.

Hyper-links

Google Docs automatically creates hyper-links for email addresses and website URLs.

For more go to www.elluminetpress.com or email office@elluminetpress.com

To insert a hyper-link for anything else, first select the word or text with your mouse.

For more click here

Right click on your selection, then select 'link' from the popup menu.

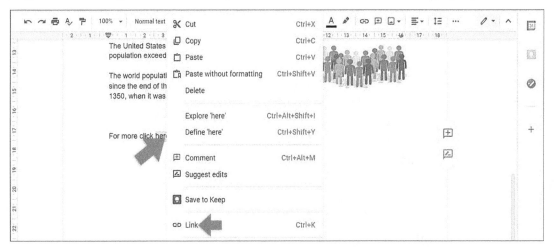

Enter the URL of the website you want to link to, then click 'apply'.

To remove a hyper-link, just right click on it, then select 'remove link' from the popup menu.

Equations

Google Docs includes a feature for displaying equations correctly and has some very common ones built in.

$$Speed = \frac{Distance}{Time}$$

$$Volume = \frac{4}{3}\pi r^3$$

To build an equation, go to your insert menu and select 'equation'.

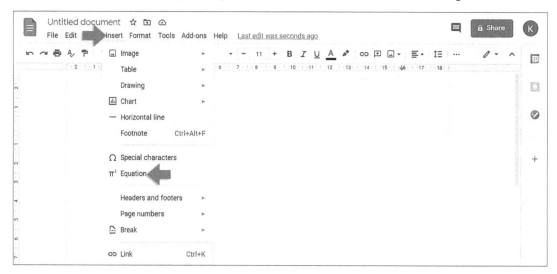

An equation toolbar will appear. Here, you'll find five groups of symbols you can use to create your equations.

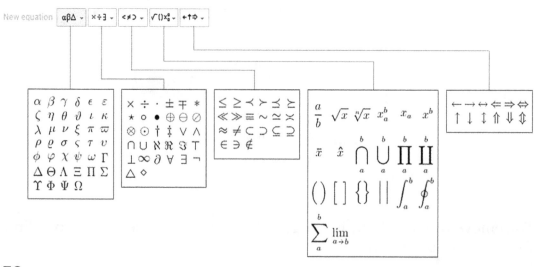

We can start building our equation. In this example, we're creating the formula for calculating the volume of a sphere. First type

```
volume =
```

Then we need to insert a fraction, so from the equation templates, select the 'mathematical operators' group, then click 'a/b'.

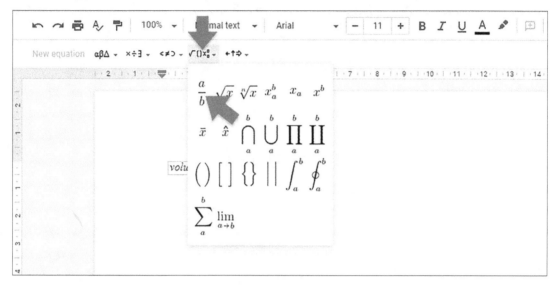

Then type 4 at the top, press the tab key on your keyboard, they type 3 at the bottom. Press the tab key again to move on.

$$volume = \cdot \quad volume = \frac{4}{3}$$

Now we need to insert a symbol for Pi. So from the Greek letters group select Pi (π).

$$volume = \frac{4}{3}\pi$$

Next, we need to enter r^3. To do this, select the 'mathematical operator' group on the equation toolbar, then click x^b.

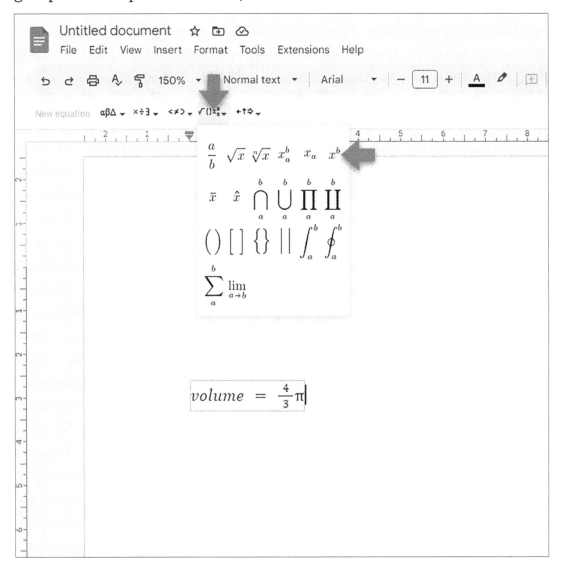

Type in r, press tab, then type in 3.

$$volume \ = \ \frac{4}{3}\pi r|$$

You'll end up with your equation.

$$volume \ = \ \frac{4}{3}\pi r^3|$$

This is a very simple example to demonstrate the feature.

Page & Section Breaks

There are two types of breaks: a page break and a section break. A page break, breaks the body text of the document onto a new page.

A section break, breaks the body text and creates a new section in the document with different formatting, page orientation, margins, headers & footers, and page numbering.

There may be occasions where you need to force a new page. Perhaps you are writing a report and you need to start a new chapter. Instead of pressing the return key until a new page is created, you should insert a page break.

You may need to insert a section break if, for example, you are writing a report and want to add a section for the contents pages and front matter. The reason you'd insert a section break, is so you can apply page numbering or formatting that is different to the rest of the report - perhaps Roman numeral page numbers instead of regular page numbers.

Inserting Page Breaks

To insert a page break, first click on the line in your document where you want the break.

Total annual births were highest in the late 1980s at about 139 million and is now expected to remain essentially constant at their 2011 level of 135 million, while deaths number 56 million per year, and are expected to increase to 80 million per year by 2040.

Select the 'insert' menu.

Go down to 'break', then from the slideout menu select 'page break'.

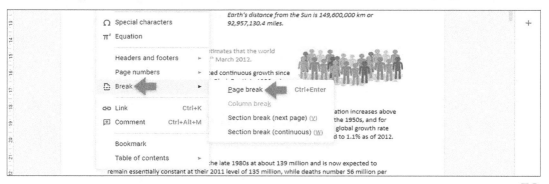

Inserting Section Breaks

To insert a section break, first click on the line in your document where you want the break.

> Total annual births were highest in the late 1980s at about 139 million and is now expected to remain essentially constant at their 2011 level of 135 million, while deaths number 56 million per year, and are expected to increase to 80 million per year by 2040.

Select the 'insert' menu. Go down to 'break', then from the slideout menu select 'section break (next page)' or section break (continuous).

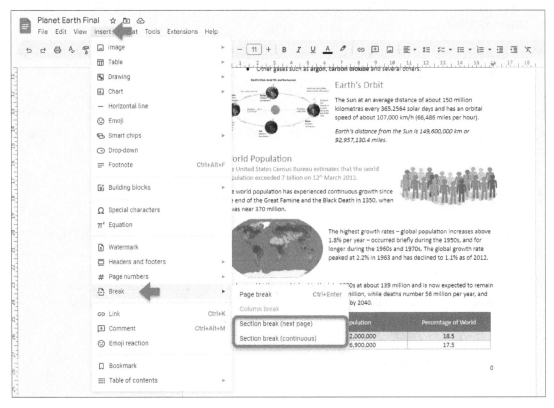

What's the difference? Well, a 'continuous section break' starts the new section on the same page. A 'next page section break', starts the new section on a new page. In this example, I selected 'section break (next page)'.

> Total annual births were highest in the late 1980s at about 139 million and is now expected to remain essentially constant at their 2011 level of 135 million, while deaths number 56 million per year, and are expected to increase to 80 million per year by 2040.

Headers and Footers

Headers and footers appear at the top and bottom of a page. For example, the header on this page is "Chapter 3: Building Documents" and the footer is a page number on the bottom right.

Inserting Headers

To insert a header, select the 'insert' menu, go down to 'headers and footers', then click 'header' on the slideout menu.

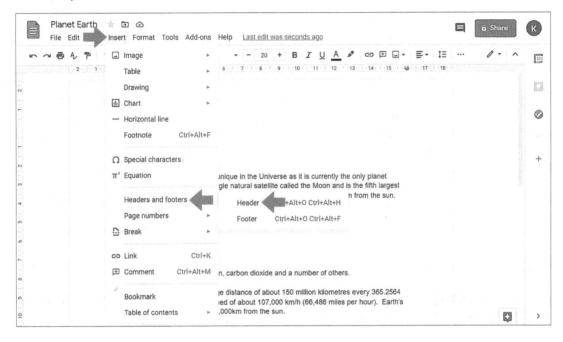

Add your page header in the top section of the screen.

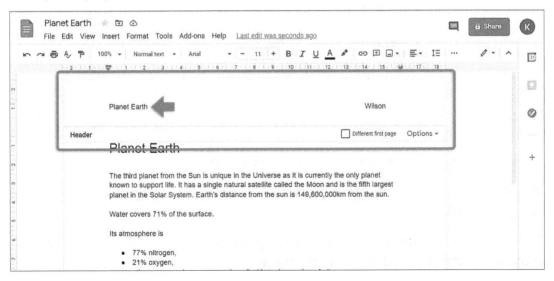

Inserting Footers

To insert a footer, select the 'insert' menu, go down the 'headers and footers', then click 'footer' on the slideout menu.

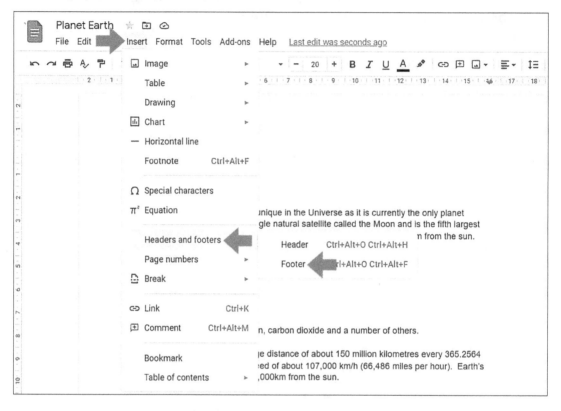

Here, you can type in your footer information in the footer section shown at the bottom of the document.

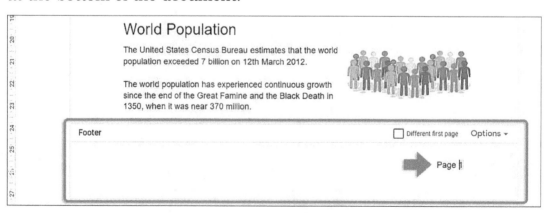

To add page numbers, click 'options', then select 'page numbers' from the popup menu.

Use the text alignment (left, centre, right), to move the footer to the left, middle, or right hand side of the page.

Formatting Headers and Footers

To format your headers or footers, first select the header or footer, then click on the 'options' menu that appears on the right hand side. From the drop down click 'format header', or 'format footer'.

Here you can change the distance of the header from the top of the page, as well as the distance of the footer from the bottom of the page.

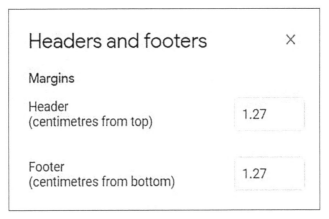

In the layout section of the dialog box, you can allow a different header for the first page of your document - useful if you have a title page that doesn't have a header or footer.

Or you can create a different header and footer on odd or even pages of your document - eg if you wanted the page number on the left on the odd pages, and on the right on the even pages.

This is useful if you're printing booklets. Here's a booklet printout with a separate header on the left for odd pages (1, 3, 5, 7, 9...)

Planet Earth

Odd page header ☐ Different first page Options ▾

Planet Earth

The third planet from the Sun is unique in the Universe as it is currently the only planet known to support life. It has a single natural satellite called the Moon and is the fifth largest planet in the Solar System. Earth's distance from the sun is 149,600,000km from the sun.

Water covers 71% of the surface.

Its atmosphere is

- 77% nitrogen,
- 21% oxygen,

And a different header on the right for even pages (2, 4, 6, 8...)

Kevin Wilson

Even page header Options ▾

The United States Census Bureau estimates that the world population exceeded 7 billion on 12th March 2012. The world population has experienced continuous growth since the end of the Great Famine and the Black Death in 1350, when it was near 370 million.

Click 'apply' on the dialog box to apply any changes to your document. Here below on the left, is an odd page (page 1) and on the right, an even page (page 2). Notice where the headers are.

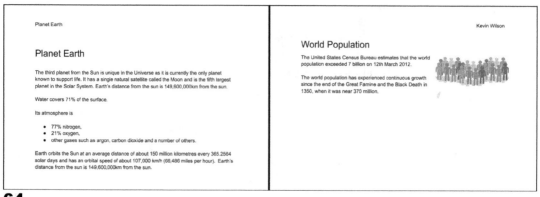

Footnotes

Click the position in the document where you want to insert a footnote.

Click the 'insert' menu, then select 'footnote'.

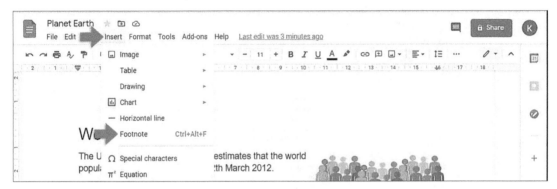

In the section that appears at the bottom of your document, type your footnote.

Here, you can see the footnote added to the bottom of the page.

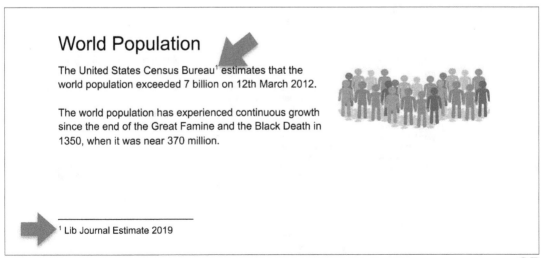

Creating Columns

Adding columns to your document arranges your text in a similar fashion to a newspaper. To add columns, click on the 'format' menu, then go down to columns. Select a pre-set from the slideout menu

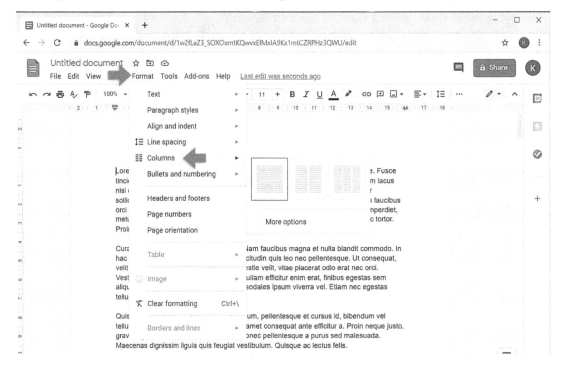

If you want to create custom columns, click 'more options'. In the 'column options' dialog box, enter the number of columns (1, 2 or 3), set the size of the gap between the columns in 'spacing', then select whether you want to add a line between the columns or not.

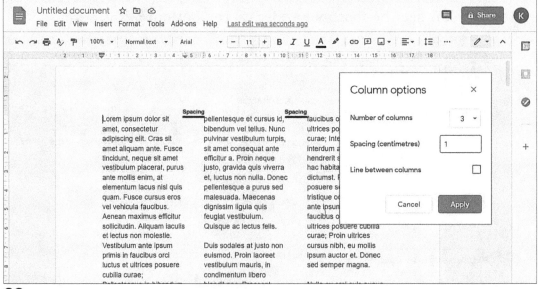

Contents Pages

The contents tool works by scanning your document for heading styles. For example, Title, Heading 1, Heading 2, Heading 3 and so on. So in the example below we see 'planet earth' is marked as 'heading 1', 'earth's orbit' is marked as 'heading 2'.

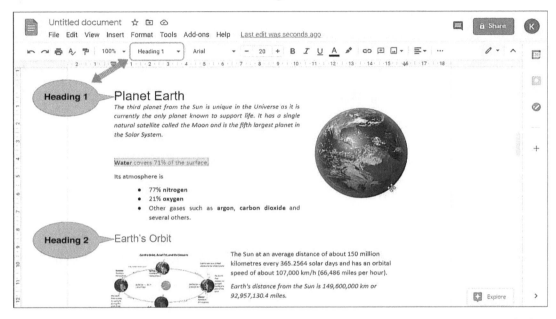

To create a table of contents, create a blank page at the start of the document - to do this, go to the top of the page and insert a page break. Add the title 'contents' to the page. Next, click the 'insert' menu, go down to 'table of contents'. Select either contents with page numbers, or contents without page numbers.

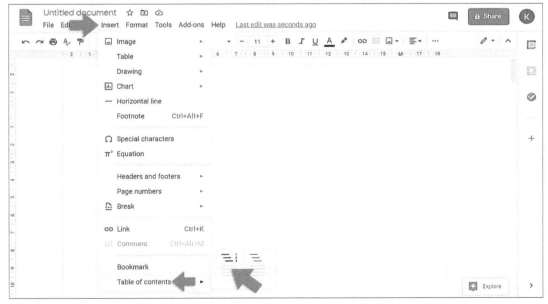

Once the table of contents has been generated, it will appear below your title

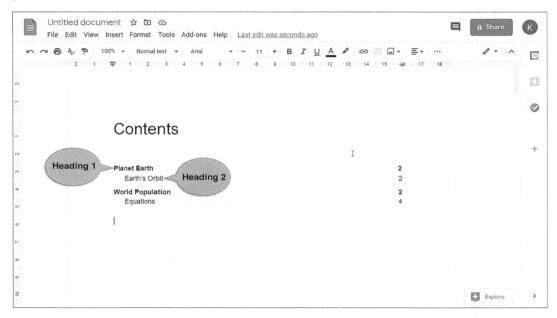

You can click on the links in the table of contents to edit the link or font.

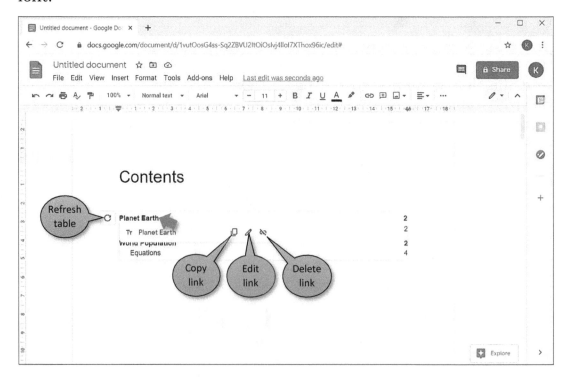

Here, you can refresh the table of contents - if you've added pages or edited your document. You can also copy a link, edit and delete links to pages.

Emojis

An emoji is a small digital image or icon that represents an idea, emotion, or concept. Emojis are often used in electronic communication, such as text messages, social media posts, and email, to convey feelings or emotions that might be difficult to express in words alone.

To insert an emoji, place your cursor where you want to insert the emoji in your document. Go to the 'insert' menu then select 'emoji'.

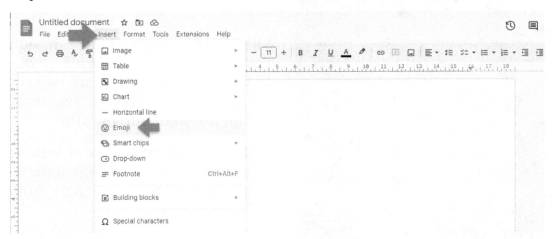

From the popup window, select the 'emoji' category from the drop-down menu. Then click on the emoji you want to insert.

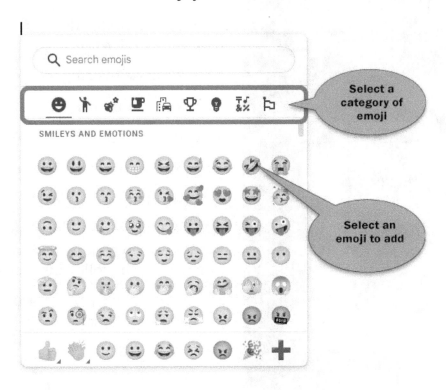

4

Adding Images & Graphics

With Google Docs, you can add pictures from Google Drive, your device, directly from your camera if you're using a tablet, phone or laptop, the web, and by URL

In this section we'll take a look at adding graphics to your documents - how to upload and insert from various sources.

We'll also take a look at formatting, resizing and cropping images, as well as adjusting the text wrap.

We'll go through adding drawings, diagrams and WordArt.

- Adding & Resizing Images
- Rotate an Image
- Cropping Images
- Wrap Text around Images
- Drawings

Have a look at the video resources section. Open your web browser and navigate to the following website.

e l l u m i n e t p r e s s . c o m /
images-googledocs

Adding Images

Adding images to your document is easy. There are six ways you can add photos:

- Your Google Drive - any photos you've uploaded or saved to Google Drive
- Your Google Photos - any photos you've taken on your phone or laptop that have been saved into the Google Photos App
- By URL - a link to an image on a website
- Search the web - using Google Image Search
- Upload from your computer - upload a photo saved on your device.
- Camera - taken directly from the camera on your phone or tablet.

From Google Drive

To add an image from your Google Drive, click the 'insert' menu

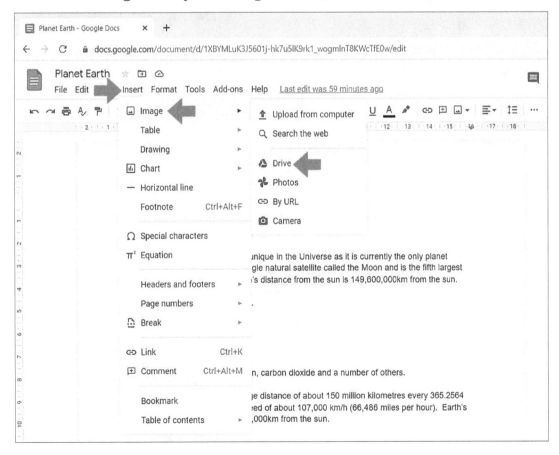

Go down to 'image', then select 'drive' from the slideout menu.

Chapter 4: Adding Images & Graphics

From the Google Drive panel on the right hand side, click 'my drive', then navigate to and select the image you want. Click 'insert'.

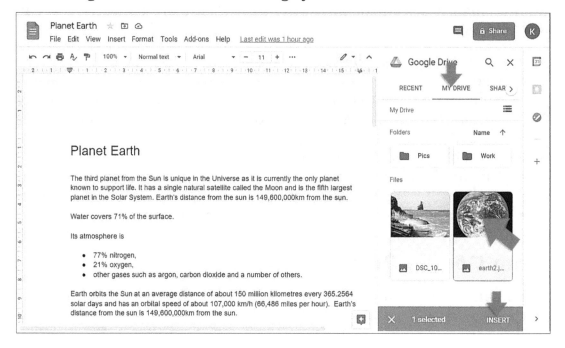

Google Photos

To add an image from your Google Photos, click the 'insert' menu.

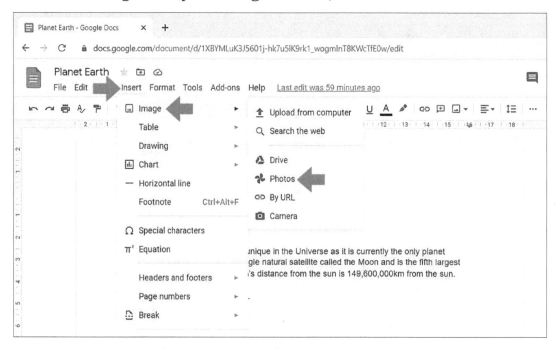

Go down to 'image', then select 'photos' from the slideout menu.

Browse through your photos or albums in the panel on the right hand side, click on the photo you want to add, then click 'insert'.

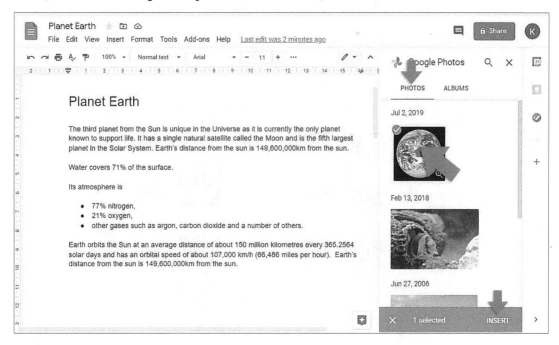

Upload from PC

If you have a photo on your Mac, PC or laptop, you can upload and insert it into your document. To do this, click the 'insert' menu, go down to 'images', select 'upload from computer' in the slideout menu.

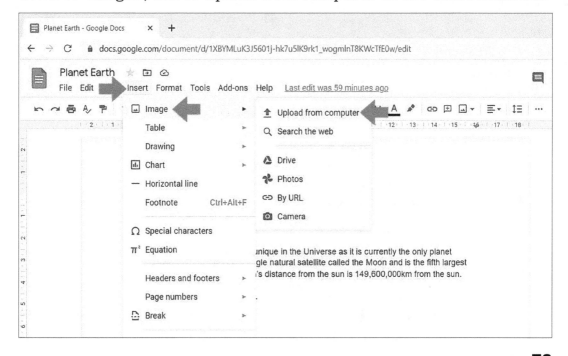

In the dialog box that appears, navigate to and select the photo you want to upload and insert. Then click 'open'.

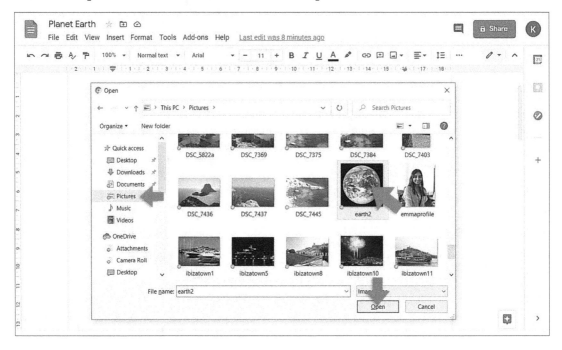

Web Search

You can search for images using Google Image Search. To do this, click the 'insert' menu, go down to 'images', select 'search the web' in the slideout menu.

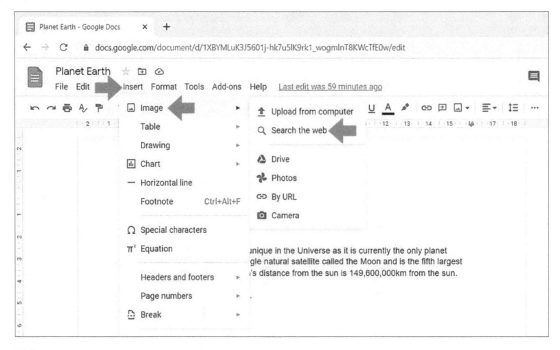

In the panel on the right hand side, enter your Google search in the search field at the top

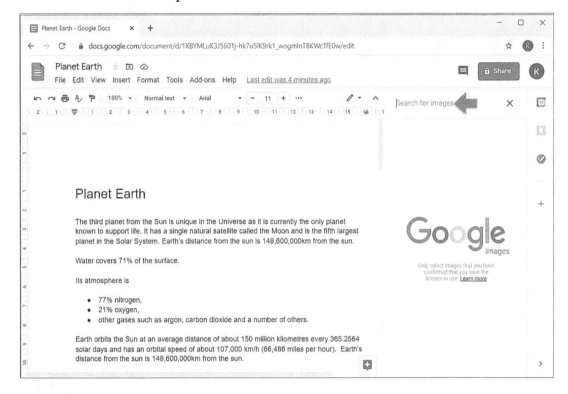

Select an image from the search results, then click 'insert'.

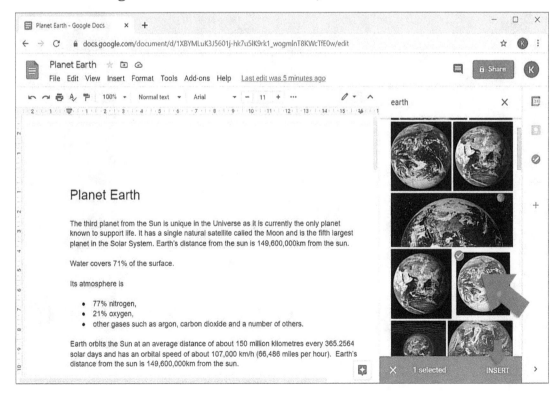

Camera on Laptop

If you are using Google Docs on a laptop/chromebook with a camera, you can insert a photo directly from the onboard camera. To do this, click the 'insert' menu, go down to 'images', select 'camera' from the slideout menu. Click 'allow' to allow access to your camera if prompted by your browser.

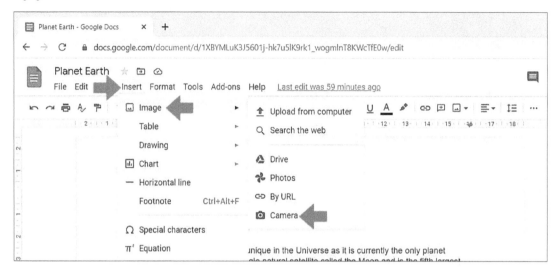

In the window that appears, line up the subject in the frame, then click the yellow capture icon at the bottom.

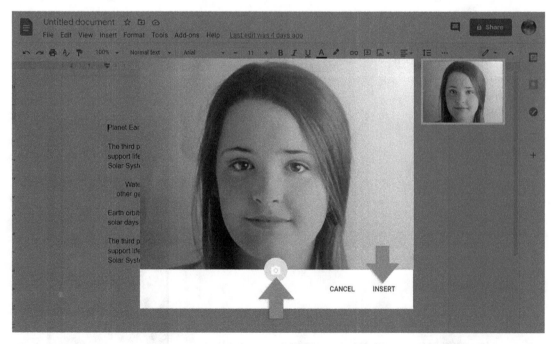

Select a photo from the right if you've taken more than one, then click 'insert'.

Camera on Tablet/Phone

If you are using Google Docs on a tablet (eg iPad) or phone, select the + icon on the top right. Go down to 'image', then tap 'from camera'. Tap 'allow' on any security prompts that may appear.

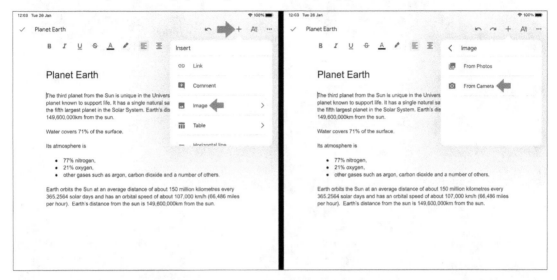

Take the photo with your camera.

Chapter 4: Adding Images & Graphics

Tap 'use photo' on the bottom right to insert the photo into your document.

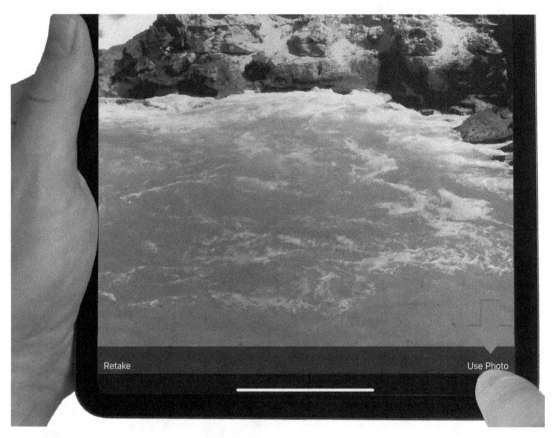

The photo will appear in your document.

Resize Images

If you've inserted an image, you may need to resize it. See adding images on page 71. To resize, click on the image. Around the edges of the image, you'll see some resize handles.

To resize the image, click and drag these handles. The best way is to click and drag one of the corner handles to resize the image.

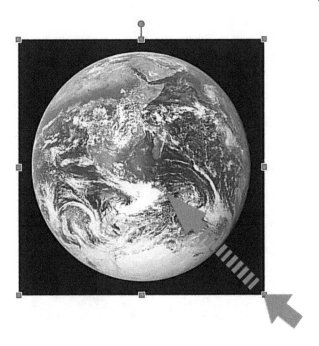

This will help prevent the image from becoming squashed or stretched

Rotate an Image

To do this, click on the image. At the top of the image, you'll see a rotate handle.

To rotate the image, click and drag the rotate handle to the right to rotate clockwise, drag left to rotate counter-clockwise..

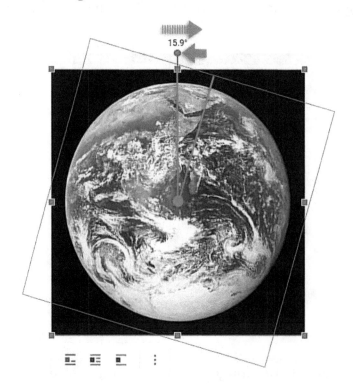

Cropping Images

If you insert an image into your document, and it has unwanted parts, or you want to concentrate on one particular piece of the picture, you can crop the image. First, insert an image into your document. See adding images on page 71.

To crop, click on the image, then select the 'crop' icon from the toolbar.

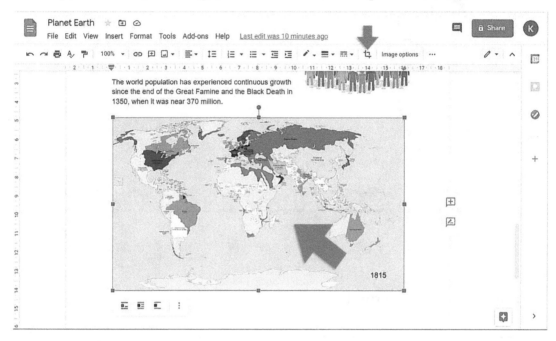

If you look closely at your image, you will see crop handles around the edges, circled below.

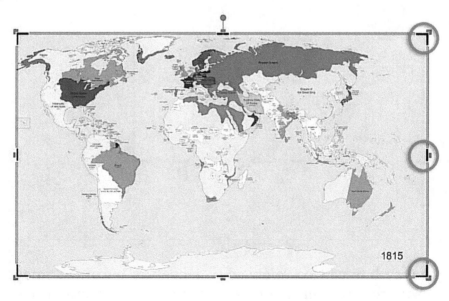

Click and drag these handles around the part of the image you want to keep. Eg, I just want to show Africa in the image. Start with the bottom right.

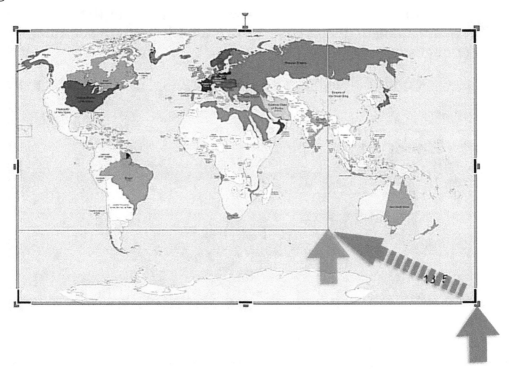

Do the same with the top left.

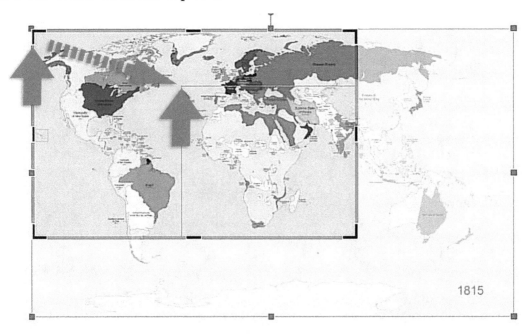

The light grey bits will be removed to leave the bit of the image inside the crop square. Press enter on your keyboard to execute the crop.

Wrap Text around Images

When you insert an image, the image will be inserted in-line with the text, meaning the image is on a line of text, as you can see below.

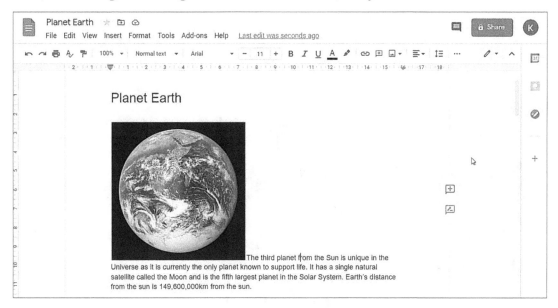

The document would flow much better if you wrapped the relevant text around the image. To change the text wrap, click on the image. You'll see icons appear along the bottom left

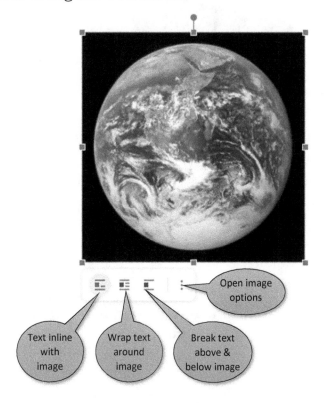

Chapter 4: Adding Images & Graphics

To wrap the text around the image, select the wrap text icon.

Set the margins - the gap around the top, right, bottom and left sides of the image.

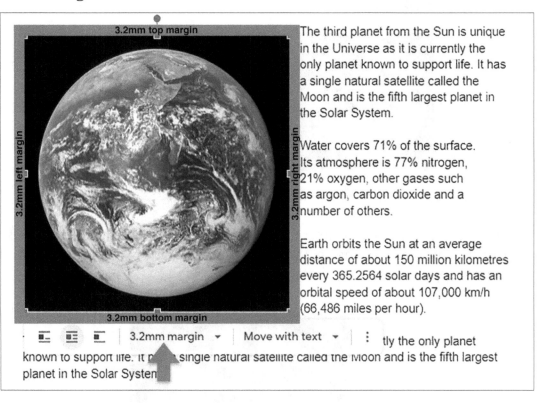

In the position options, you can choose between 'move with text' and 'fixed position on page'.

'Move with Text' means the image will move up or down with the paragraph it is aligned to if you add or delete text above the image.

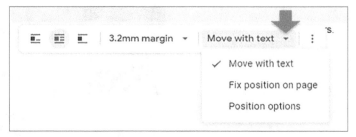

'Fix Position on Page' means any text added won't affect the position of the image, the image will remain in the position it was inserted, regardless if you add or delete text above the image.

Drawings

Drawings is a diagramming tool that allows you to import images, insert shapes, arrows, scribbles, text and wordart from pre-designed templates. To insert a drawing, select the 'insert' menu, then go down to drawings. Select 'new' from the slideout menu.

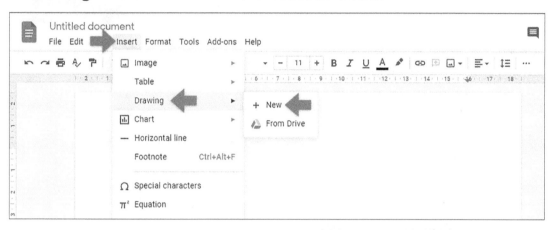

You'll see the drawing canvas window appear. Here you can create your drawings. Along the top of the window, you'll see some controls. Lets take a look at what they do.

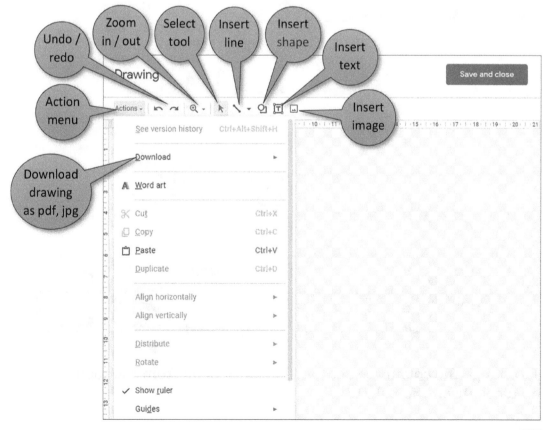

WordArt

WordArt is useful for creating titles. First open a new drawing as shown on page 85 if you haven't already done so. Click on the 'action menu', then select 'wordart'. In the field that appears, type in your title.

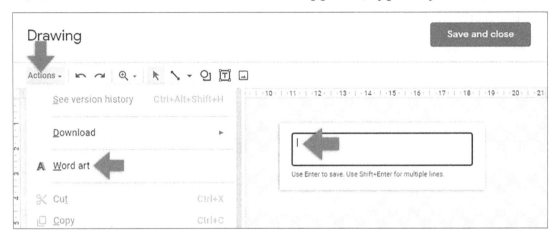

Click on your wordart to select it.

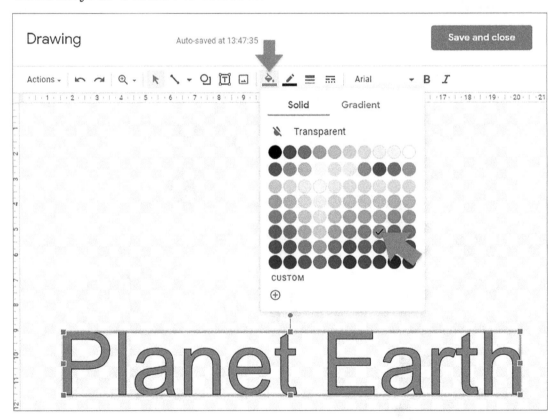

To change the colour, select the 'fill colour' icon from the toolbar. Click on a colour on the palette.

To change the outline, select the 'border colour' icon from the toolbar

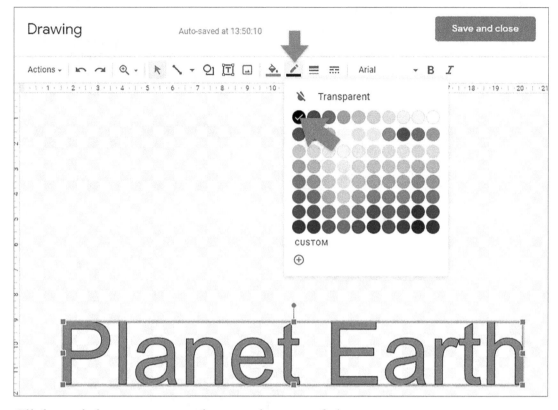

Click and drag your wordart to the top of the canvas.

Shapes

To add a shape, first open a new drawing as shown on page 85 if you haven't already done so. Select the 'shapes' icon from the toolbar, go down to 'shapes', 'arrows' or 'call outs', then select a shape you want to add from the slideout menu.

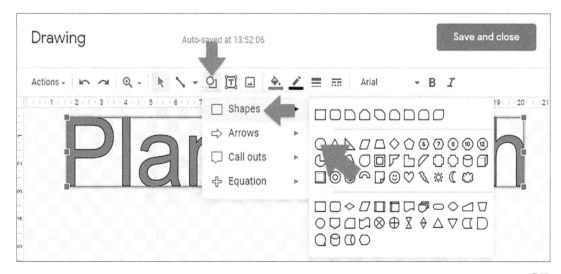

Click and drag the shape onto the canvas to set the size. To make a perfect circle or square, hold down the shift key.

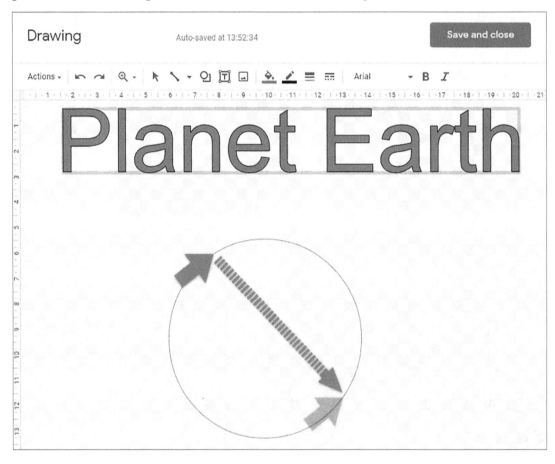

To change the fill colour, click the 'fill colour' icon, then select a colour.

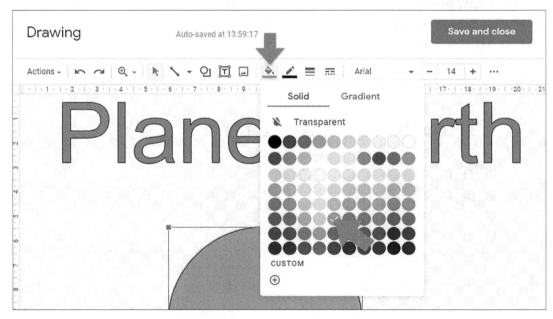

To change the border colour, click the 'border colour' icon, then select a colour

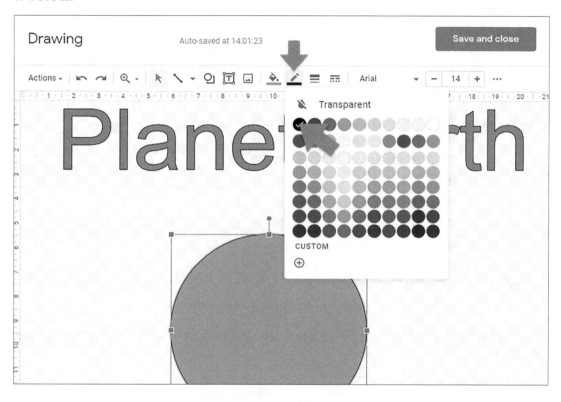

If you want to change the border thickness, click the 'borders' icon, then select a thickness from the slideout menu.

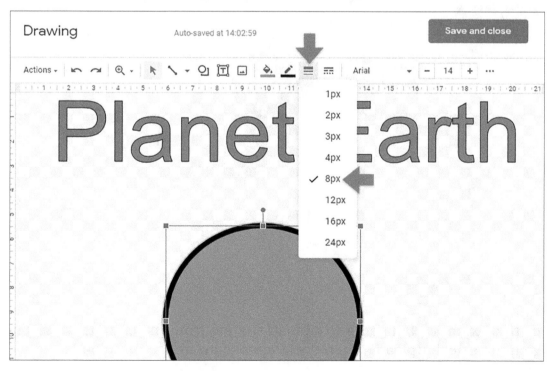

Images

You can insert images and photos into your drawings. To add an image, first open a new drawing as shown on page 85 if you haven't already done so. Select the image icon from the toolbar.

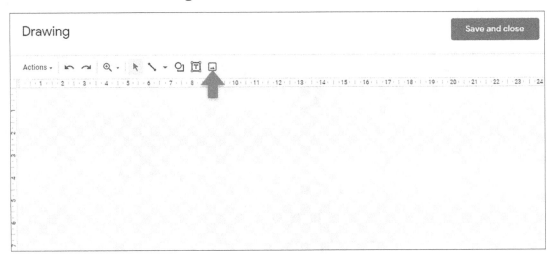

From the four tabs along the top of the screen, select where your image is stored.

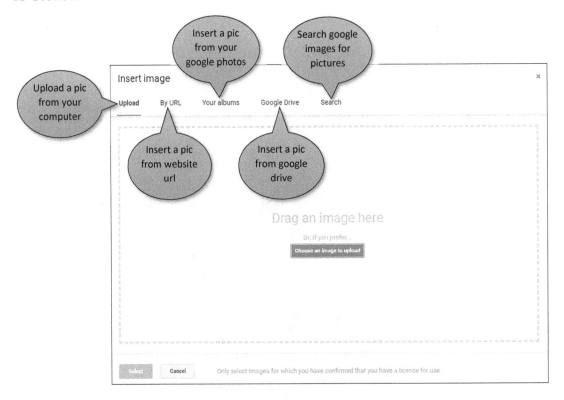

In this example, I'm going to upload the pic from my computer, so I'm going to select 'upload'. Then click 'choose an image to upload'.

Browse to and select the image you want to insert.

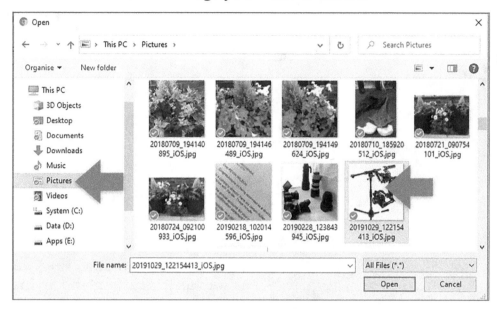

Now, you can insert shapes and other objects. For example, below, I've added a callout bubble to label the camera and stand. To learn how to insert shapes see page 87.

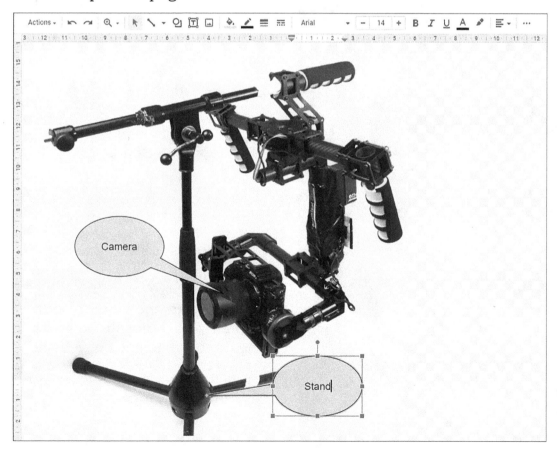

5

Tables and Charts

In this section, we'll take a look at creating tables and adding charts to our documents.

We'll go through inserting tables, as well as formatting and laying out a table.

We'll also take a look at inserting various types of charts to illustrate statistics and data in your documents. You can add pie charts, line graphs, and bar or column charts.

- Adding Tables

- Formatting Tables

- Borders, Cell Shading

- Split and Merge Cells

- Adding Charts

- Formatting Charts

- Customising Chart

Have a look at the video resources section. Open your web browser and navigate to the following website.

e l l u m i n e t p r e s s . c o m /
charts-googledocs

Tables

We have added some more text about world population to our document. Now we want to add a table to illustrate our text.

Inserting Tables

To insert a table, click on your document where you want the table to appear. In this example, I want it to appear just below world population paragraph.

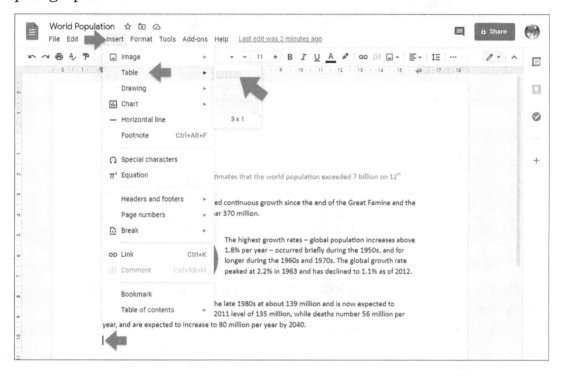

Click on the 'insert' menu, go down to 'table'. From the slideout, select the number of rows and columns you want in your table using the grid. Here, in the example below, I've selected a table with 3 columns and 4 rows.

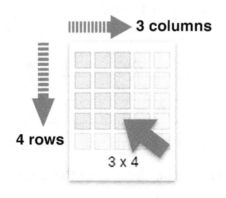

Chapter 5: Tables and Charts

You can now enter the data into your table. Press tab to move to the next cell, or click in the cell you want.

World Population

The United States Census Bureau estimates that the world population exceeded 7 billion on 12th March 2012.

The world population has experienced continuous growth since the end of the Great Famine and the Black Death in 1350, when it was near 370 million.

The highest growth rates – global population increases above 1.8% per year – occurred briefly during the 1950s, and for longer during the 1960s and 1970s. The global growth rate peaked at 2.2% in 1963 and has declined to 1.1% as of 2012.

Total annual births were highest in the late 1980s at about 139 million and is now expected to remain essentially constant at their 2011 level of 135 million, while deaths number 56 million per year, and are expected to increase to 80 million per year by 2040.

Country	Population	Percentage of World
China	1,372,000,000	18.5
India	1,276,900,000	17.5
USA	312,793,000	4.35

If you run out of rows, select the last cell on the bottom right, then press the tab key on your keyboard.

Country	Population	Percentage of World
China	1,372,000,000	18.5
India	1,276,900,000	17.5
USA	312,793,000	4.35

A new row will be inserted at the end.

Country	Population	Percentage of World
China	1,372,000,000	18.5
India	1,276,900,000	17.5
USA	312,793,000	4.35

You can continue to enter the data into the table.

Text Formatting

You can format your text in the same way as any other text in your document. For example, in this table I want to make the top row bold to indicate a column heading. To do this, first select the cells

Country	Population	Percentage of World
China	1,372,000,000	18.5
India	1,276,900,000	17.5
USA	312,793,000	4.35
Indonesia	252,164,000	3.35

Select the bold icon from the toolbar.

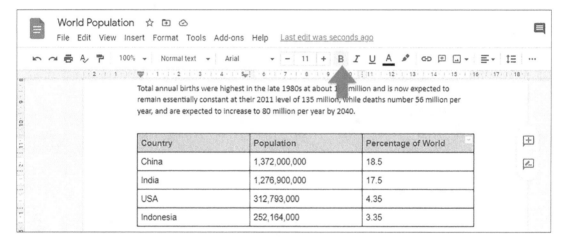

Cell Color

You can change the cell colors of any cells, rows, or columns on the table. For example, lets change the color of the cells on the top row to separate it from the rest of the table. This makes a good heading row.

First select the cells you want to format.

Country	Population	Percentage of World
China	1,372,000,000	18.5
India	1,276,900,000	17.5
USA	312,793,000	4.35
Indonesia	252,164,000	3.35

Chapter 5: Tables and Charts

Click on the 'format' menu, then go down to 'table'. Select 'table properties' from the slideout menu

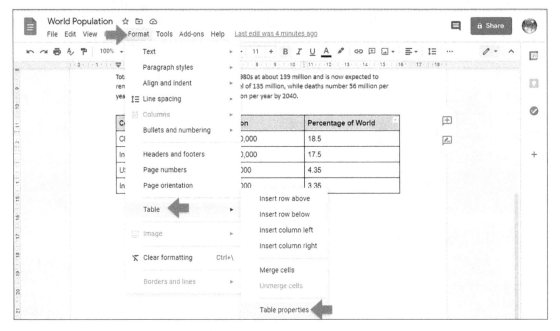

On the right hand side of the screen, select the 'color' tab. Select 'cell background color', then choose a color from the palette.

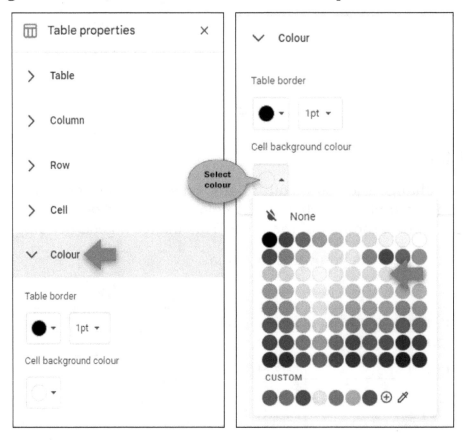

Borders

To change the borders of the whole table, select the table, then click the 'format' menu, go down to table, then click 'table properties'.

From panel on the right hand side of the screen, select the 'color' tab. Under 'table border', select a color from the left hand drop down box, then select a thickness from the drop down next to it.

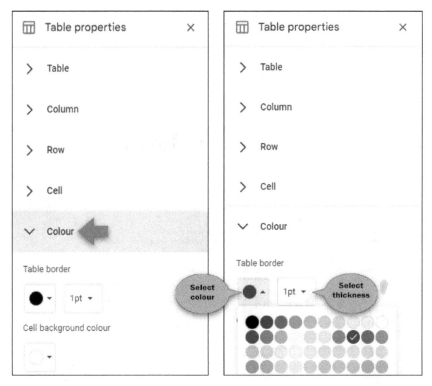

Chapter 5: Tables and Charts

To change individual borders, click on the borders on the table you want to change. If you're changing more than one border, hold down the shift key as you click each border you want to change.

For example, if I wanted to apply a thicker border to the outline of the table, I'd hold down shift, then click each of the borders on the outside of the table all the way around.

Country	Population	Percentage of World
China	1,372,000,000	18.5
India	1,276,900,000	17.5
USA	312,793,000	4.35
Indonesia	252,164,000	3.35

From the toolbar, click the border thickness icon. Select a thickness from the drop down menu.

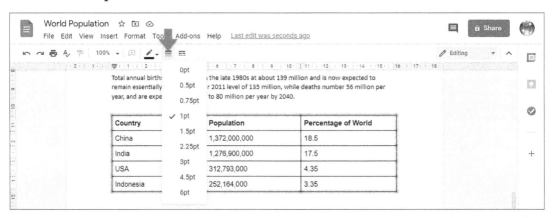

If you want to change the color, click the color icon, then select a color.

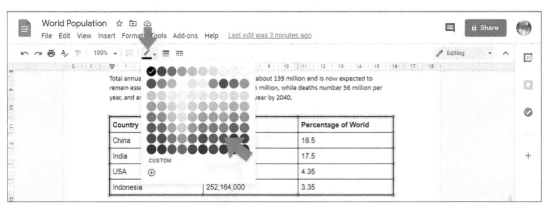

Cell Padding

Cell padding is the space between the content of a table cell and its border. It refers to the amount of space that is added within the cell, between the content and the cell's edges.

By default, a table cell in Google Docs has 0.176cm of padding, meaning that the content of the cell is 0.176 from the cell's border.

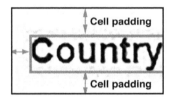

To adjust the cell padding, select the table or cells you want to format, then click the 'format' menu, go down to table, then click 'table properties'.

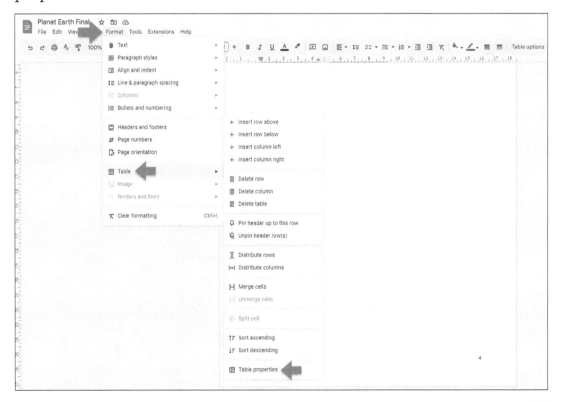

From the panel on the right hand side, select 'cell'. Adjust the 'cell padding'.

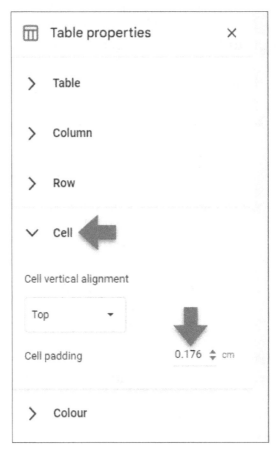

Cell Alignment

Select the data in the table, or click the cell you want to align.

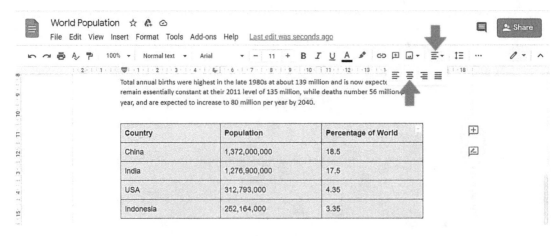

From the toolbar, select the alignment icon (left, center, right).

Split Cells

Select the cell or cells that you want to split. Right click on the cell, then select 'split cell' from the popup menu.

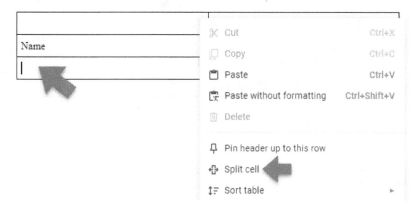

In the Split cell dialog box, choose the number of rows and columns you want to create, and click 'ok'.

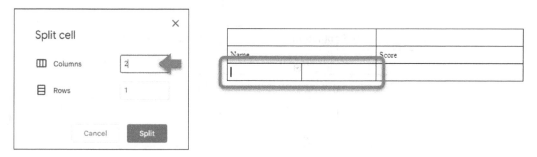

Merge Cells

Select the cells you want to merge. Right click on the selection, then select 'merge cells' from the popup menu.

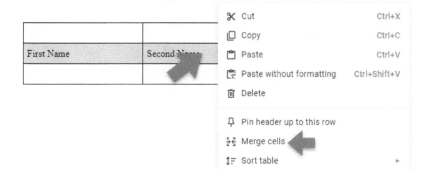

The selected cells will be merged into a single cell, and the content will be centered within the new merged cell.

Row Height

To adjust a row height, click and drag one of the row dividing lines to the up or down.

Country	Population	Percentage of World
China	1,372,000,000	18.5
India	1,276,900,000	17.5
USA	312,793,000	4.35
Indonesia	252,164,000	3.35

Column Width

To adjust a column width, click and drag one of the column dividing lines to the left or right.

Country	Population	Percentage of World
China	900,000	18.5
India	1,276,900,000	17.5
USA	312,793,000	4.35
Indonesia	252,164,000	3.35

You can also adjust all the column and row heights together using the table properties. Select all the data in the table, click the 'format' menu, go down to 'table', click on 'table properties'.

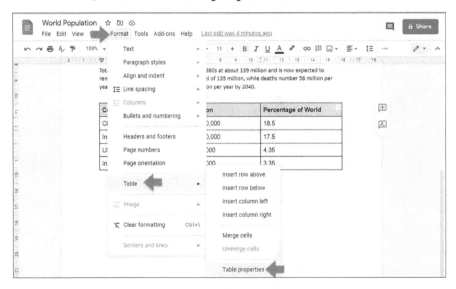

From the panel on the right hand side, open up the row and column tabs. Enter the row height and column widths into the fields shown below.

In this example, our columns are set to 5cm and the row height is 1cm.

Column width (5cm)

Row height (1cm)

Country	Population	Percentage of World
China	1,372,000,000	18.5
India	1,276,900,000	17.5
USA	312,793,000	4.35
Indonesia	252,164,000	3.35

Insert Row

In our table, lets add a row between 'india' and 'USA'.

Country	Population	Percentage of World
China	1,372,000,000	18.5
India	1,276,900,000	17.5
USA	312,793,000	4.35
Indonesia	252,164,000	3.35

Chapter 5: Tables and Charts

To do this, right click in the row 'india' is in. From the popup menu, select 'insert row below'.

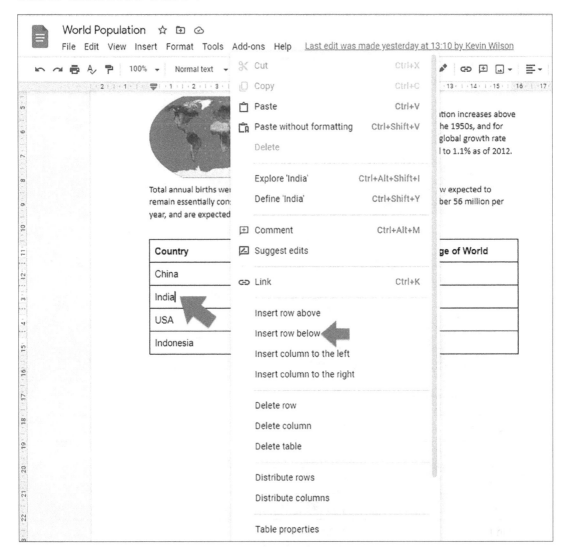

This will insert a row below the row 'india' is in - as you can see here below.

Country	Population	Percentage of World
China	1,372,000,000	18.5
India	1,276,900,000	17.5
I		
USA	312,793,000	4.35
Indonesia	252,164,000	3.35

Insert Column

In our table, lets add a column between 'population' and 'percentage of world'.

Country	Population	Percentage of World
China	1,372,000,000	18.5
India	1,276,900,000	17.5
USA	312,793,000	4.35
Indonesia	252,164,000	3.35

To do this, right click in the column 'percentage of world' is in.

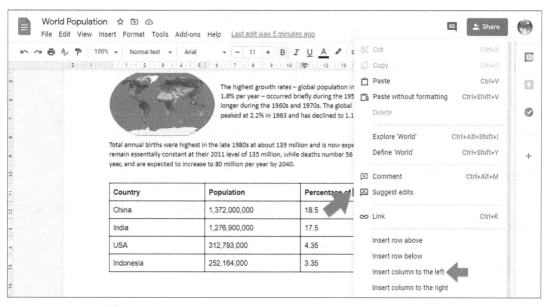

From the popup menu, select 'insert column to the left'. This will insert a column next to the column 'percentage of world' is in - as you can see here below.

Country	Population		Percentage of World
China	1,372,000,000		18.5
India	1,276,900,000		17.5
USA	312,793,000		4.35
Indonesia	252,164,000		3.35

If you wanted the column on the end, click 'insert column to the right' instead.

Delete Column

To delete a column, right click in the column you want to remove, then select 'delete column'.

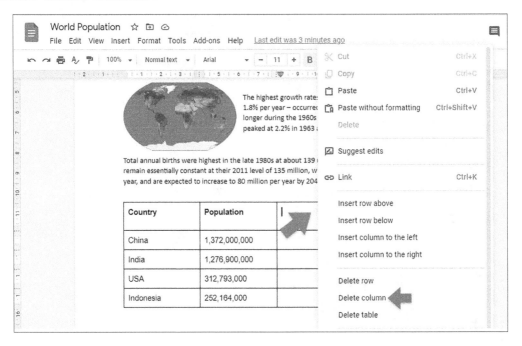

Delete Row

To delete a row, right click in the row you want to remove, then select 'delete row'.

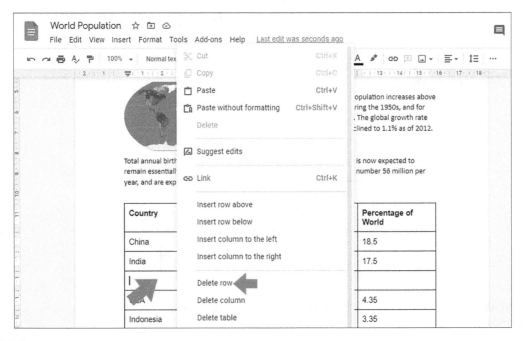

Adding Charts

You can add various charts to your documents to represent data. You can add a bar or column chart, a line graph, or a pie chart.

To add a chart, click on the location in the document you want the chart to appear, then select the 'insert' menu. Go down to chart, then select a chart type from the slidout. In this example, I'm going to add a column chart.

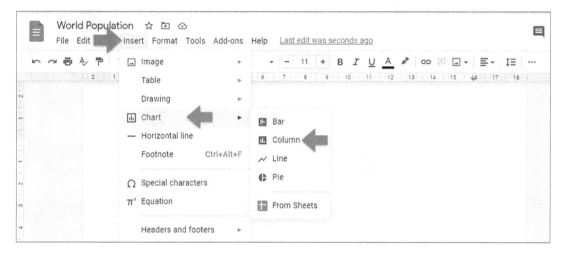

Now to enter the data, click on your chart to select it, then click the small 'link' icon on the top right.

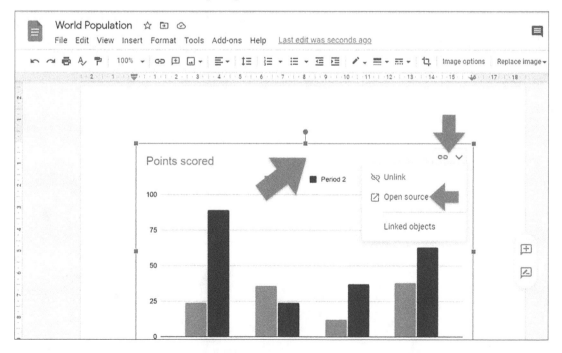

From the popup menu, select 'open source'.

Chapter 5: Tables and Charts

A spreadsheet will open up for you to enter your data. Column A is the x axis, and column B is the y axis

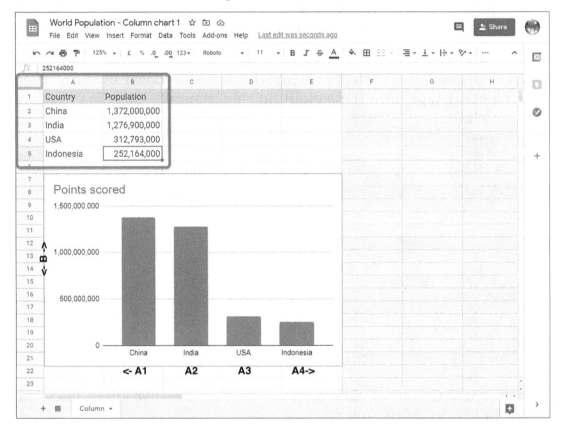

Once you've done that, make sure the spreadsheet is saved, then close the window. Go back to your document, click 'update' on your chart if it doesn't automatically update.

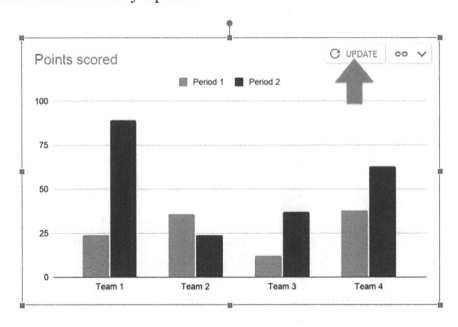

Customise your Chart

To customise your chart, click on your chart to select it, then click the small 'link' icon on the top right. Select 'open source' from the popup menu.

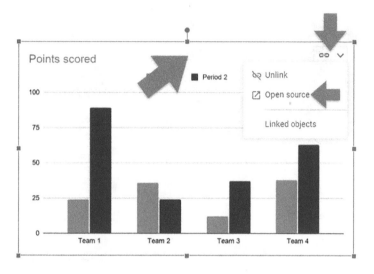

Your chart will open up in a spreadsheet. Click on your chart to select it, then click the three dots icon on the top right.

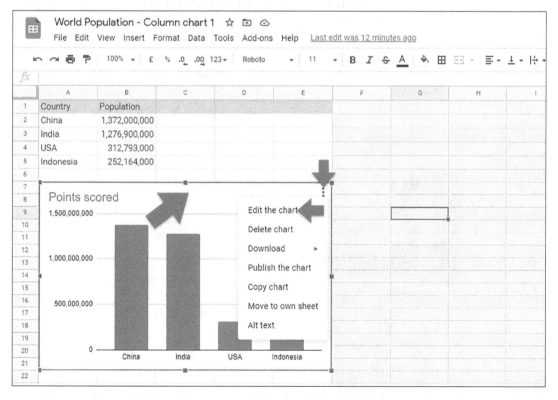

Select 'edit the chart'.

Chapter 5: Tables and Charts

You'll see the chart editor panel appear on the right hand side.

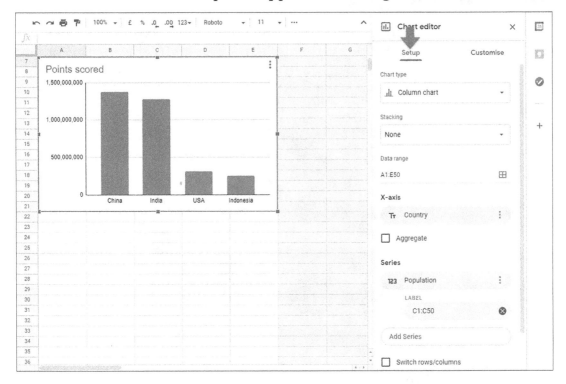

Here, you can start to customise your chart. From the 'setup' tab you can change the chart type (pie chart, column chart, line chart, etc). You can also add a data series and range for your chart.

From the 'customise' tab you can change the look and feel of your chart.

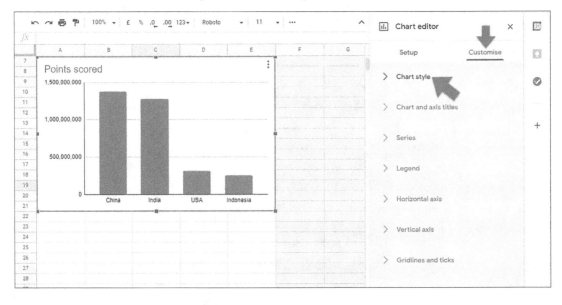

To do this, select one of the sections from the 'customise' tab to expand the customisation options.

Chart Style

You can change the chart style - background color, border color, 3D effect, and font.

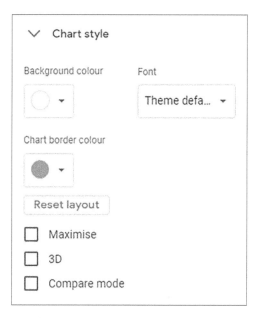

Chart & Axis Titles

You can change the chart title, as well as the horizontal and vertical axis labels - just use the 'chart title' drop down menu.

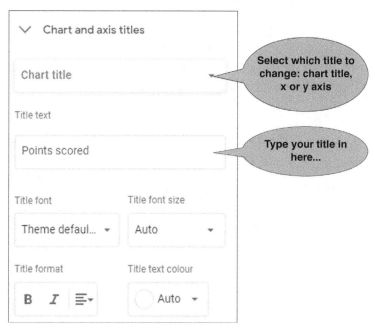

Here, you can also change the font and text color using the controls at the bottom of the section.

Data Series

In the 'series' section, you can change the bar colors, as well as add data labels to the bars on your chart or add a trend line

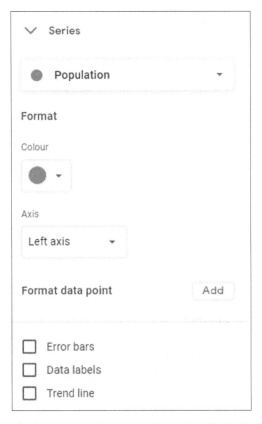

To format individual bars (or data points), click 'add' next to 'format data point', select the data point (or bar on your chart) you want, then select a color from the color palette.

In the 'legend' section, you can add and format your chart legend.

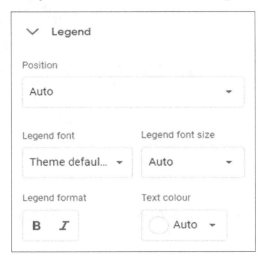

Horizontal Axis

In the 'horizontal axis' section, you can format your horizontal axis labels, etc.

Vertical Axis

In the 'vertical axis' section, you can format your vertical axis labels, etc.

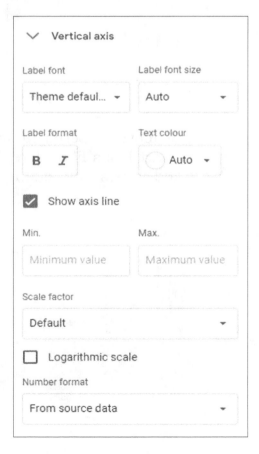

Gridlines and Ticks

In the 'gridlines and ticks' section, you can adjust the scales and spacing for each axis. As well as add gridlines to make your chart easier to read.

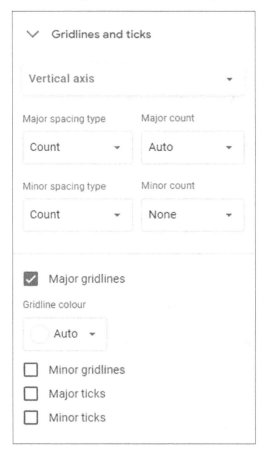

Using the sections described above, experiment with some of these settings and see what your chart looks like. Here, I've added a chart title, added labels to the x and y axis, and changed the color of the chart.

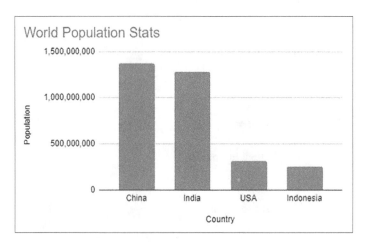

Download & Publish Chart

You can download a chart as a PNG or PDF. To do this click on your chart to select it, then click the small 'link' icon on the top right. Select 'open source' from the popup menu.

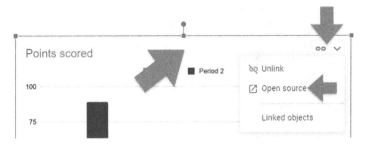

Your chart will open up in a spreadsheet. Click on your chart to select it, then click the three dots icon on the top right. To download the chart, go down to 'download', then select PNG to download the chart as an image.

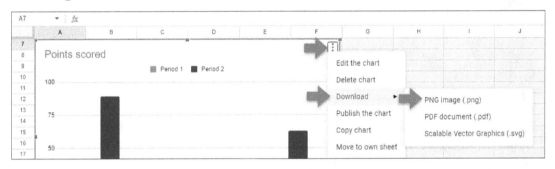

If you want to publish the chart to the web - ie create a link to send to other people, click the three dots icon on the top right of the chart, select 'publish the chart'. Click 'publish'.

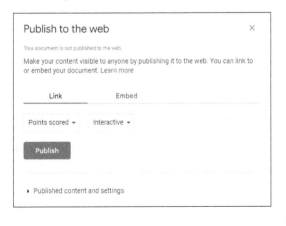

You can copy and paste the highlighted link into an email or message.

6 Sharing and Collaboration

One of Google Docs main advantages is it's sharing and real-time collaboration features.

This means you can share a file with others allowing them to edit the document and add to the project.

You can also communicate with your co-editors, see which changes have been made, and add comments.

In this section, we'll go through document collaboration. We'll find out how to share a document with other users, how to comment, edit, and work on a document with other people.

- Sharing a Document
- Accepting the Invitation to Collaborate
- Editing Shared Documents
- Sharing a Link
- Restricted Links
- People without Google Accounts
- Stop Sharing a File

Have a look at the video resources section. Open your web browser and navigate to the following website.

e l l u m i n e t p r e s s . c o m /
sharing-googledocs

Sharing a Document

In this demo, lets share a document with two other users who will be collaborating on it. The setup is as follows. I will be sharing a document from my laptop with Sophie on her chromebook and Claire on her tablet.

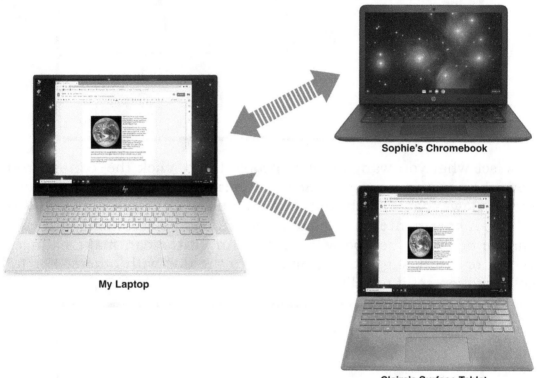

Sophie's Chromebook

My Laptop

Claire's Surface Tablet

These devices could be anywhere in the world that has an internet connection.

To share a document, first open the one you want to share, then click the 'share' icon on the top right.

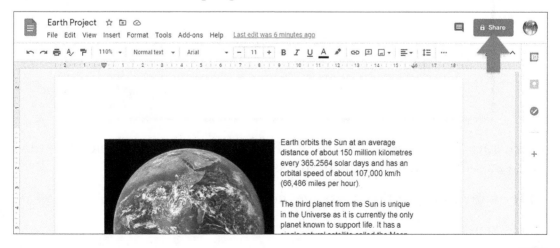

In the field at the top of the window, enter the email addresses of the people you want to share the document with. In this demo, I'm sharing my doc with Claire and Sophie, so I'd type in their email addresses.

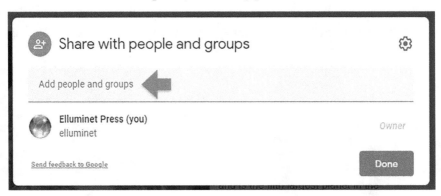

Now set what you want to allow people to do, click the 'editor' drop-down box on the top right. Select a permission from the drop down box. A **viewer** can view the doc, but can't make changes or share it with others. A **commenter** can make comments and suggestions, but can't change or share the doc with others. An **editor** can make changes, accept or reject suggestions, and share the doc with others. For full collaboration set it to 'editor'.

Make sure 'notify people' is ticked. If you enable 'notify people', all email address will be included in the message.

Enter a message, in the 'message' field.

Click 'send'.

Accepting the Invitation to Collaborate

If someone has shared a document with you in Google Docs, go to your email and open the invitation. Here on Claire's surface tablet, is the invitation to the document that was shared with her from my laptop in the previous section. Just click on the 'open in docs' button. This will open the shared document.

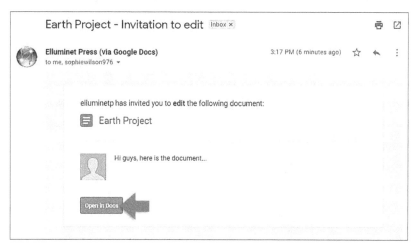

The document will open in Google Docs were you can edit the document, or write comments and chat with other users.

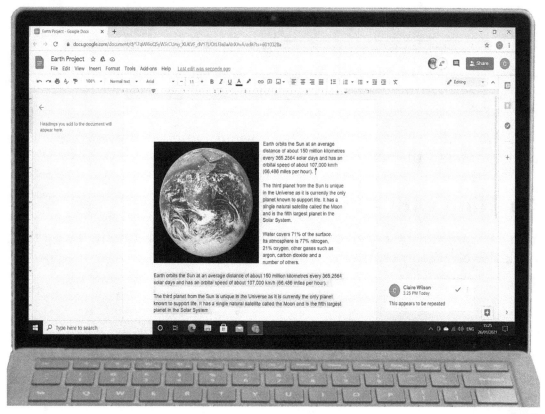

Editing Shared Documents

All the user's you've shared the document with can work on it together.

Making Edits

When you're working on a shared document, you'll see each person's edits marked with their username.

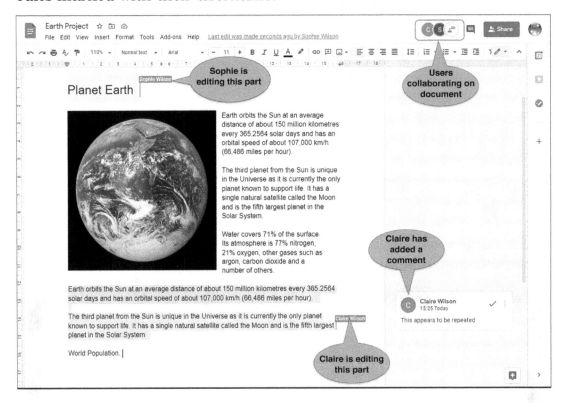

You can edit the document as normal, and see everyone else's contributions - they can see the same.

Chatting with Other Collaborators

You can chat to the other users working on your document. To do this, click the chat icon on the top right.

Use the chat window on the right hand side, enter your message in the field at the bottom right.

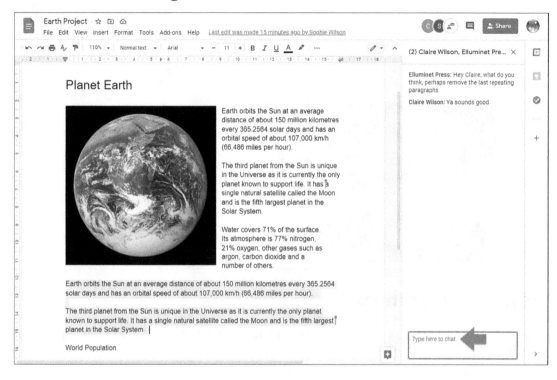

Making Comments

You can also comment on any part of the document. To do this, select the part of the text, then click the blue '+' comment icon that appears on the right hand side.

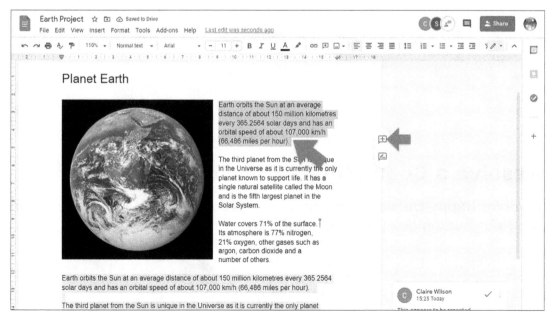

Enter your comment in the field on the right hand side. Click 'comment' to post your comment.

Reply to Comment

If you want to reply to a comment, click on it in the side bar on the right hand side.

Enter your comment in the text field, then click 'reply' to post.

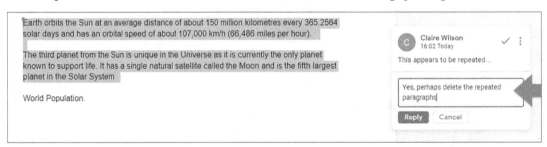

Resolve a Comment

If you're happy the comment has been resolved, click the tick icon on the right hand side of the comment box.

Making Suggestions

This feature works like Microsoft Word's track changes function, where you can see the changes made by other users. The suggestion feature allows you to make changes to the Doc that other users can then accept or reject the changes.

To start, you'll need to go into 'suggesting' mode. To do this, click the 'edit mode' icon on the top right. Select 'suggesting' from the drop down menu.

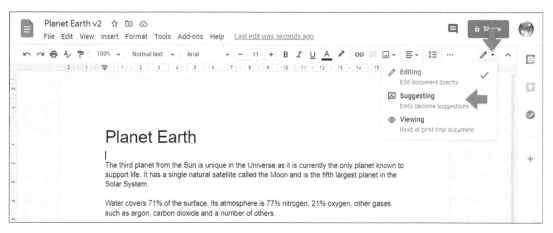

Now make your suggestions. For example, I'm going to suggest a different layout for the second paragraph in the example above.

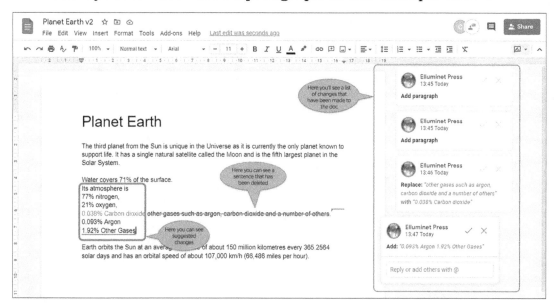

Everything a user types in under suggesting mode, appears in green text with a corresponding comment box on the right hand panel, that allows users with 'editor' share permissions to accept, reject or reply to the suggestion.

To comment on a suggestion, click on it in the right hand panel, then type your comment into the text field.

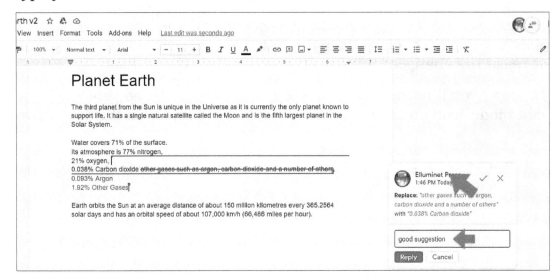

To accept the suggestion, click on the 'tick' icon on the comment box in the right hand panel.

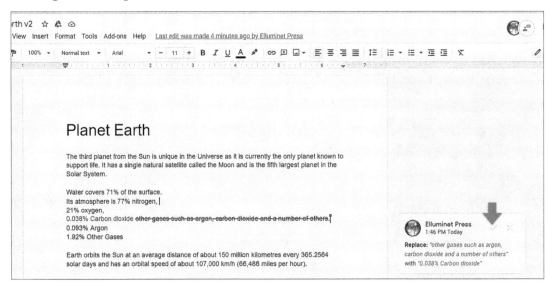

To reject a suggestion click the 'x' icon.

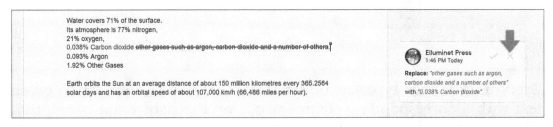

This will remove the suggestion and return to the original text.

Sharing a Link

You can share a link with someone who may or may not even have a Google account. To do this open the document you want to share, then click the 'share' icon on the top right.

Sharing a Link with Anyone

Sharing a link with anyone means as it's name suggests, anyone who has the link can view the document. This is not the most secure way to share a file with someone, so don't use it to share documents with sensitive information.

Click 'change to anyone with link' in the bottom section.

Google Docs will generate a link for you.

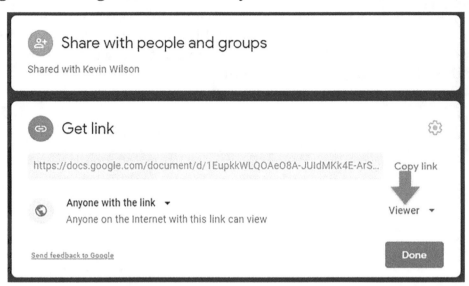

Set the 'view' permissions. Click on the 'viewer' drop down box, then select an option. If you want the person to just view the document, select 'viewer'. If you want the person to be able to edit the document, select 'editor'.

Click 'copy' to copy the link to your clipboard.

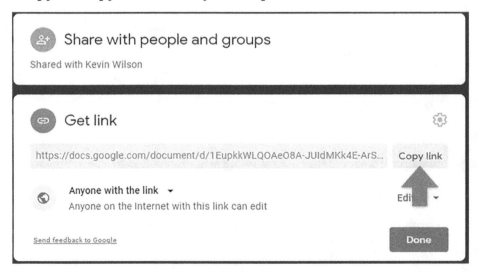

Paste the link into an email or message to send to the person you want to share with. Type a message, then press CTRL - V on your keyboard to paste in the link.

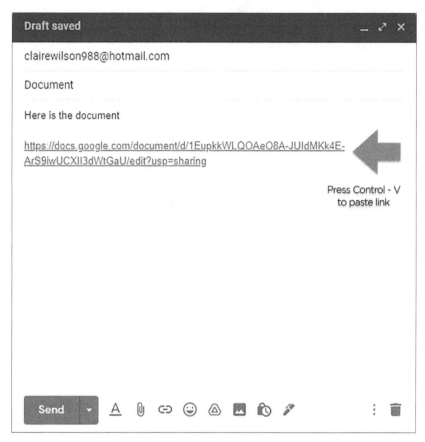

Click 'send' when you're done.

Restricted Links

To generate a link to send to people you've shared a document with, click the 'share' icon on the top right.

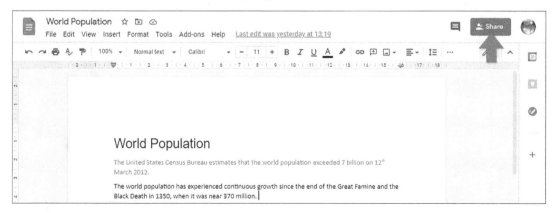

You'll see a list of people along the top the document has been shared with. Click 'change' in the bottom section.

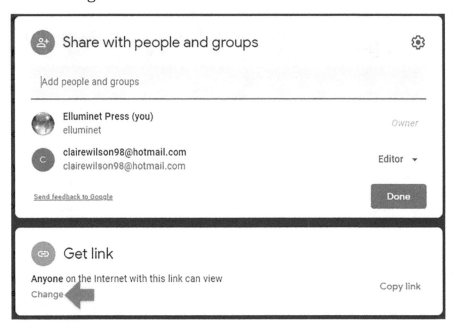

From here, click 'anyone with a link' and change it to 'restricted'.

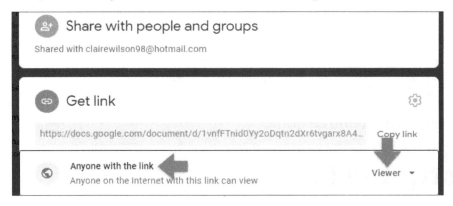

If you want to invite the person to edit the document, select the drop down box on the right, change from 'viewer' to 'editor'.

Click 'copy link' on the right hand side, then click 'done'. Paste the link into an email or message.

People without Google Accounts

Sharing a link publicly might not be the best option. If the person doesn't have a Google Account, you can still share the file with them. To do this, open the file then click the 'share' icon on the top right.

Enter the person's email address in the top field and press enter on your keyboard.

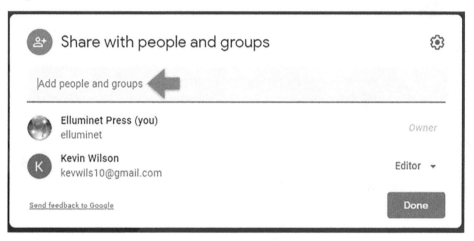

Add a message, then select the permission from the drop down box on the right hand side. Set it to 'editor' if you want this person to be able to edit the document.

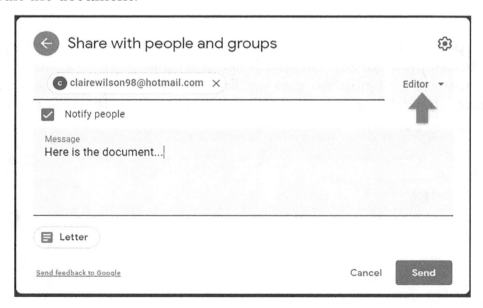

Click 'send', then select 'share anyway' if prompted.

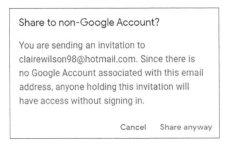

When the other person checks their email, they'll receive an invitation. To view the document, click 'open in docs'.

If the person doesn't have a Google Account, they'll need to sign up for one before they can edit the file. When the other person opens the file, they will see a 'sign in' or 'sign up' link on the top right of the screen. To sign up, click 'sign up to edit' and follow the on-screen instructions.

Stop Sharing a File

To stop sharing a file, first open it, then click the 'share' icon on the top right.

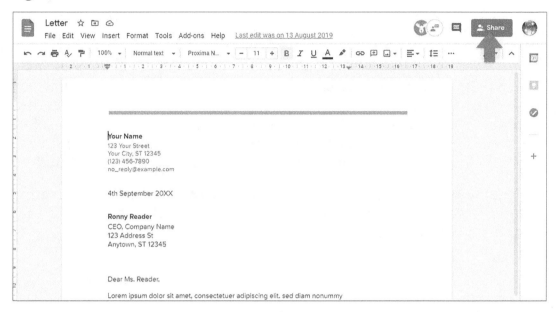

From the 'share with people and groups' section, click the drop down box next to the person you want to remove.

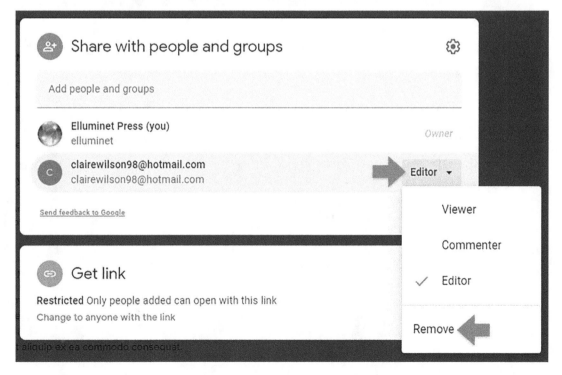

Select 'remove' from the drop down menu. Click 'save' when you're done.

Smart Chips

A Smart Chip is an interactive tag that displays additional information about a specific person, document, or topic. They make it really easy to reference other people, files, dates, or calendar events. This allows you to add context to your document by mentioning other people, files, and topics from within your document.

To use Smart Chips in Google Docs, you can simply type "@" followed by the name of a person or a file, and Google Docs will suggest relevant matches from your Google Drive or Google Contacts. You can then select the desired match, and Google Docs will automatically create a link to that person or file, which can be clicked on to access more information.

For example, in the following document, Claire and I are collaborating on a document. Lets say I want to reference another document that contains a chart for this section.

Total annual births were highest in the late 1980s at about 139 million and is now expected to remain essentially constant at their 2011 level of 135 million, while deaths number 56 million per year, and are expected to increase to 80 million per year by 2040.

Country	Population	Percentage of World
China	1,372,000,000	18.5
India	1,276,900,000	17.5
USA	321,793,000	4.35
Indonesia	252,164,800	3.35
Brazil	204,878,000	2.77

To reference the document, first type in an at sign @. You'll see a popup menu appear.

You can also go up to the 'insert' menu and select 'smart chips'.

Then type in the name of the document. Keep in mind that the document will need to be saved to your Google Drive. Select the document.

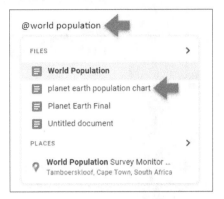

Now when your collaborators hover their mouse pointer over the smart chip, they'll see a link to the file, to which they can request access.

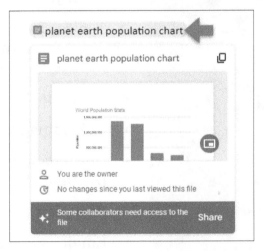

You can also add people, dates, and places.

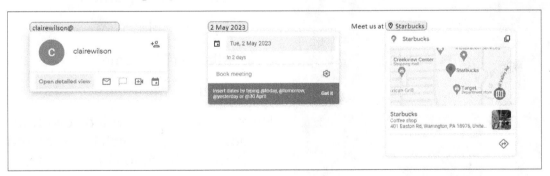

Smart chips are a useful tool to save time and improve collaboration, allowing users to easily reference and share relevant information from other apps without having to switch between different tabs or applications.

7

Managing Documents

In this section, we'll take a look at how to save and open documents, convert them to other formats, and how to print them out if you need a hard copy.

We'll also take a look at page and print setup, print margins, and how to scale printouts to paper sizes.

- Opening Documents

- Uploading Documents

- Downloading & Converting Documents

- Printing Documents

- Email as Attachment

- Document Translation

- Define & Lookup

- Spelling & Grammar

- Add Ons

Have a look at the video resources section. Open your web browser and navigate to the following website.

e l l u m i n e t p r e s s . c o m /
managing-googledocs

Opening Documents

If you're already working on a document, you can open another using the 'file' menu. Just select 'open'.

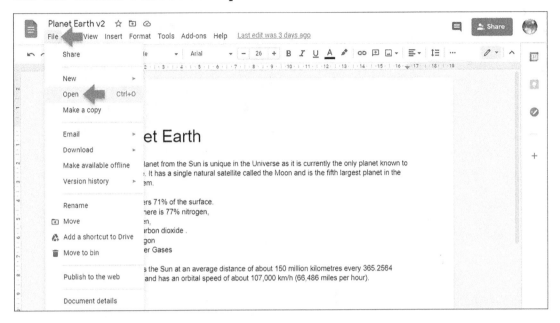

From the 'open' dialog box, navigate to 'My Drive', then select the document you want to open.

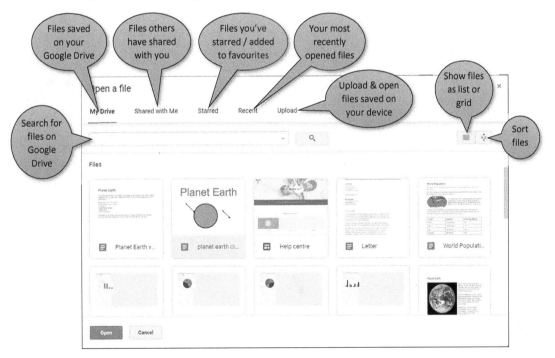

Click 'open' on the bottom left of the dialog box.

If you're opening a document from the home screen, click the 'file picker' icon on the right hand side of the screen.

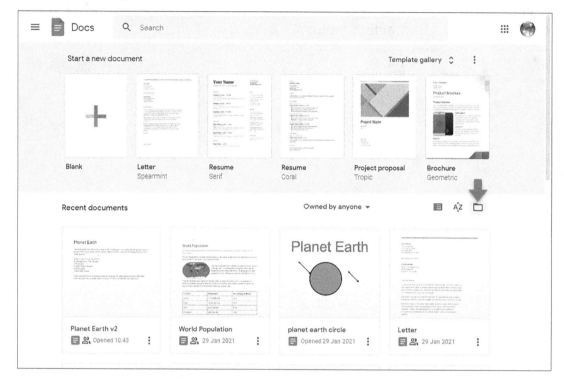

Select the 'My Drive' tab, then click on a file to open.

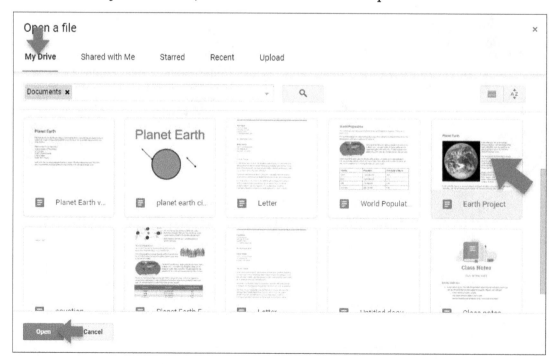

Click 'open' when you're done.

Uploading Documents

If you have a document saved on your PC, Mac or Laptop, you can upload it

To upload a document, click on the 'file picker' icon on the right hand side of the home screen.

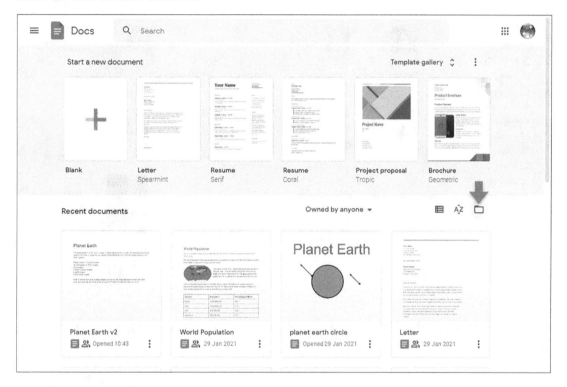

Select the 'upload' tab, then click 'select a file from your device'.

Chapter 7: Managing Documents

Select a document. As we're uploading to Google Docs, you should upload a microsoft word document (.doc or .docx), text file (.txt), or a rich text file (.rtf).

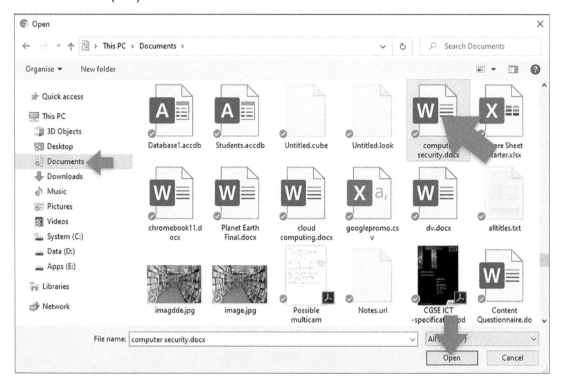

If you've uploaded a Microsoft word document, Google Docs will convert it for you.

Downloading & Converting Documents

If you need to save your document for Microsoft Word, or a PDF, you can do this using the 'document download' feature. This is useful if you want to send someone the document who uses Microsoft Word, or if you need to send a report to someone as a PDF.

First open the document you want to convert and download. Select the 'file' menu, then go down to 'download'.

Select the format you want from the slideout menu.

- Use 'microsoft word' if you want to convert and download the document as a word document.

- Use 'opendocument format' if you want the document to be compatible with various word processors, such as Word Perfect, Apache OpenOffice or LibreOffice.

- Use 'rich text format' if you want maximum compatibility with other word processors. RTF is a universal document format and is compatible with most word-processing packages.

- Use 'PDF document' if you want to send a read-only version of the document such as a sales report to someone else.

- Use 'web page' if you want to convert the document to an HTML document for a website.

- Use 'epub publication' if you are writing an ebook and want to read the document on e-readers such as kindle, google books, nook and other e-book readers.

In this example, I'm going to export this document as a PDF.

Navigate to the folder on your PC, laptop or mac; give the document a name. Here, in the example below, I'm saving this document into my 'documents' folder.

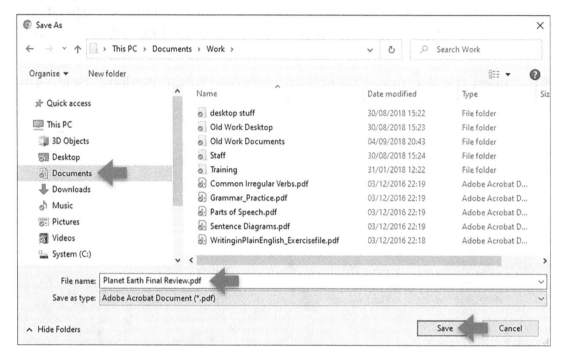

Click 'save'.

Printing Documents

Once you're finished writing your documents, you might need to print them. To do this, make sure your printer is connected and online.

Page Setup

If you need to change the page orientation, paper size, page margins, or page colour, you can do that here. Once you have a document open, go to the file menu, on the top left. Select 'print setup'.

From here, you can change the page orientation: landscape or portrait. You can change the paper size: select A4, letter, legal, etc

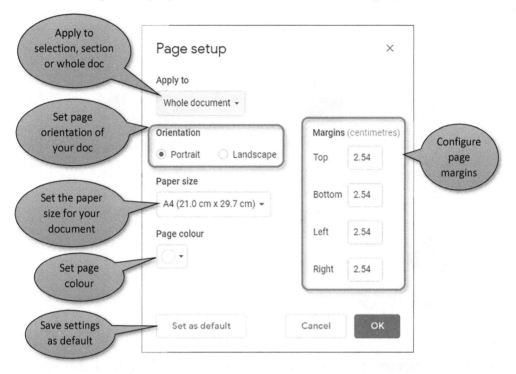

You can set the margins for your document and choose a page colour.

Click the drop down box under 'apply to'. Here, you can select what part of your document you want to apply the page setup settings to.

Chapter 7: Managing Documents

Use the 'apply to' setting at the top of the dialog box to apply these settings to a section of your doc if you've split your document using section breaks.

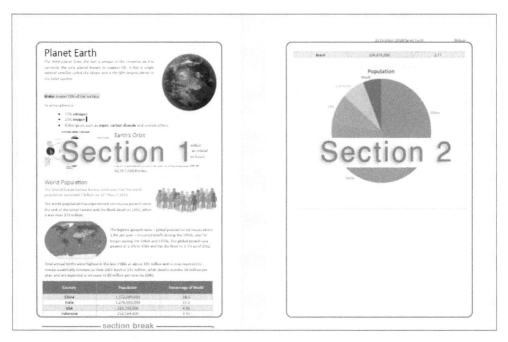

Or if you've selected part of your document - highlighted the text with your mouse.

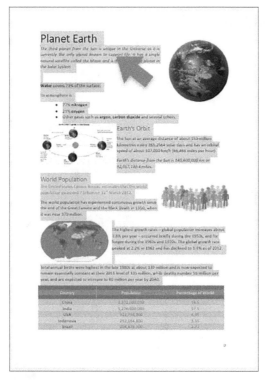

Or the whole document...

Print

To print your document, click the 'file' menu on the top left, then select 'print' from the drop down menu.

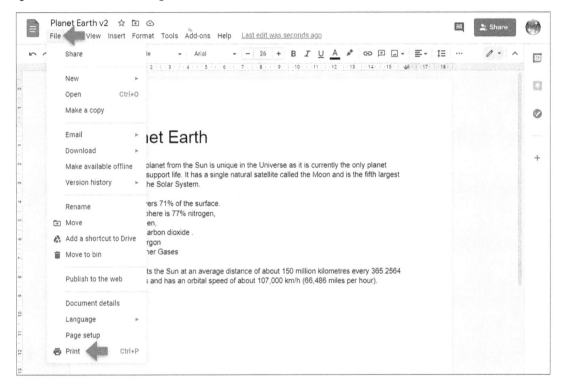

From the dialog box that appears, select your printer from the 'destination' drop down selection box.

In the 'pages' field, set it to 'all' to print all pages in your document. If you only want to print certain pages, select 'customised' from the drop down selection box, then type in the page numbers of the pages you want to print. In this example, I'm going to print pages 1 and 4.

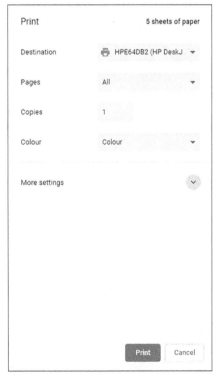

Set how many copies of the document you want, and whether you want to print the document in full colour, or just black and white.

Click 'more settings'. Here, you can change the paper size (A4, letter, legal, etc) using the 'paper size' field.

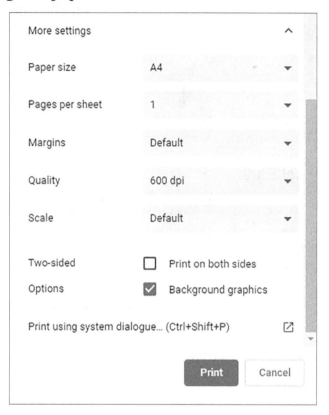

You can change the number of pages per sheet. So for example, if you wanted to put two pages on one sheet to save paper...

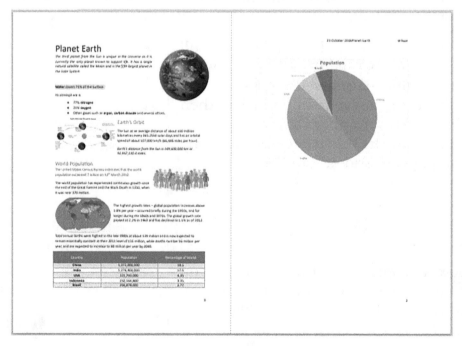

Using the 'margins' selection box, you can set your margins to 'none', 'minimum', or 'custom'. Select 'none' or 'minimum' to reduce the margins to their smallest.

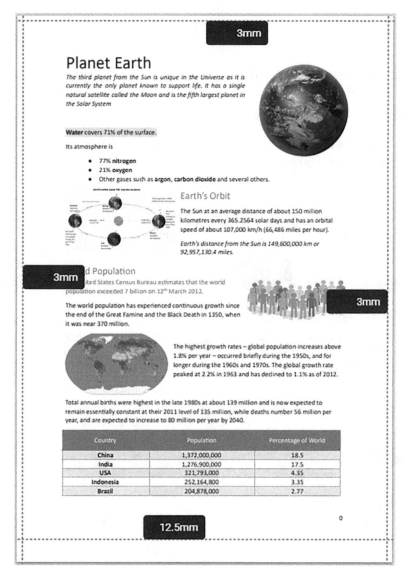

If you select 'custom', you can type in the margins. To do this, click in the margin measurement on the print preview on the left hand side of the window, then enter a new measurement. For example, below I've changed the bottom margin to 3mm.

India	1,276,900,000	17.5
USA	321,793,000	4.35
Indonesia	252,164,800	3.35
Brazil	204,878,000	2.77

12.5mm

Use the 'quality' selection box to set the quality of your print.

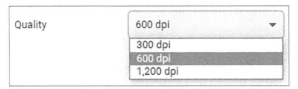

If you're printing a final copy then select a higher quality such as 600dpi or 1200dpi. However, if you're printing a quick draft and don't full quality then select 300dpi.

Using the 'scale' selection box, you can reduce or enlarge the size of a document to fit the page. Enter a percentage, eg 50% for half the size, or 125% to increase the size by 25%.

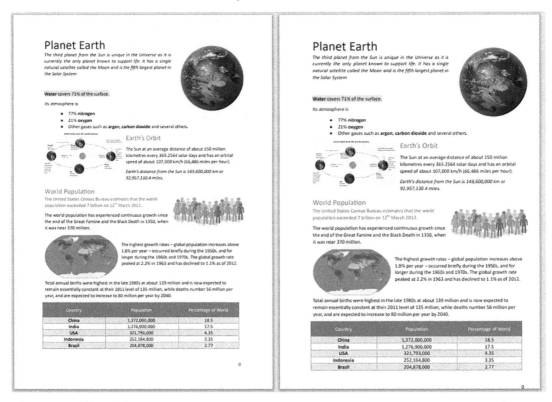

Use the 'two sided printing' option to print double sided if your printer supports this feature.

Use 'print headers and footers' to keep or remove the headers and footers if there are any on your document

'Print background graphics' doesn't apply to google docs. This is used for printing web pages that include backgrounds that you many or may not want to print.

Finally, click 'print' when you're done.

Email as Attachment

You can email your document in a variety of formats such as PDF, Word, HTML, plain text and rich text.

To do this, click on the 'file' menu, go down to 'email', then select 'email this file' from the slideout menu.

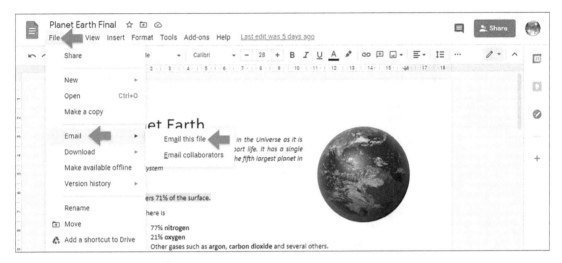

Enter the person's email address in the field at the top, add a message.

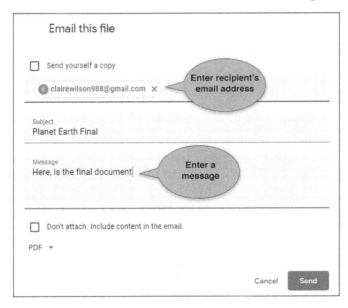

Tick "send yourself a copy" if you want to receive a copy of the email with the document attached.

Tick "Don't attach. Include content in the email" if you want to send the document as part of the email message rather than attaching it to the end.

Select the format using the drop down box on the bottom left.

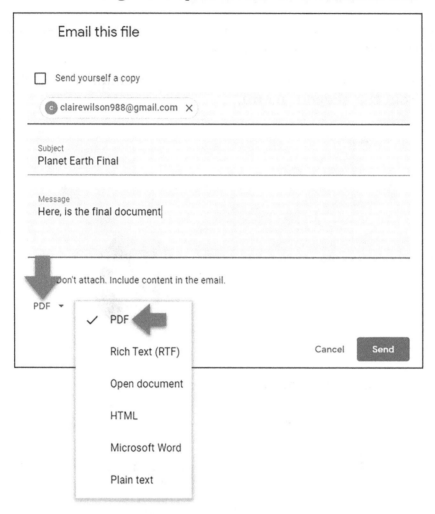

Here, you can select the format you want to send.

- PDF is useful for portability across different platforms, however the recipient won't be able to edit a PDF.

- Rich text or open document is good for compatibility between other word processors such as open and libre office.

- HTML which is useful if you want to publish your document on a website

- Microsoft word if your recipient users Microsoft Office.

- Plain text is useful if you just need the text with no formatting or images.

Select your format, then click 'send'.

Document Translation

You can translate a document into another language. While the translation is generally good enough to be understood, it's important to recognise that the translation is not perfect.

To translate a document, open the 'tools' menu, then select 'translate document'.

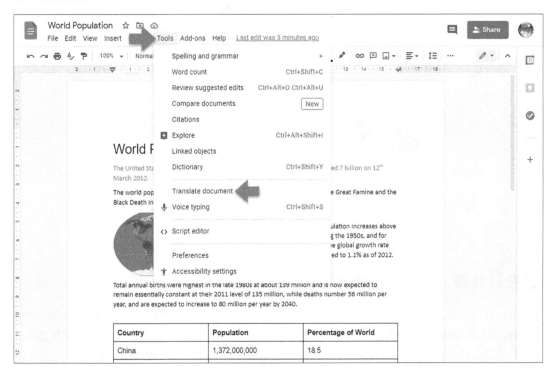

Give the document a name, then select the language you want to translate the document into, eg spanish.

Click 'translate'.

Once the translation is complete, Google Docs will create a new document for your translation

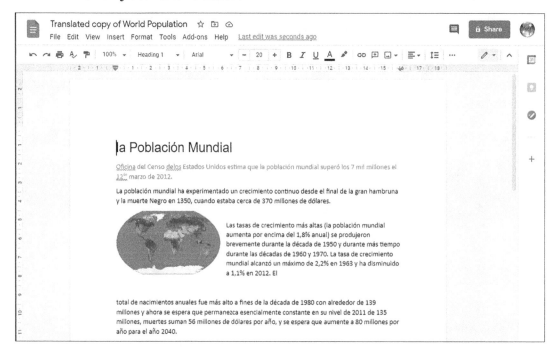

Define & Lookup

You can quickly find a definition or lookup a word in your document using the built in dictionary and Google search features. To do this, highlight a word or phrase, then right click on the selection.

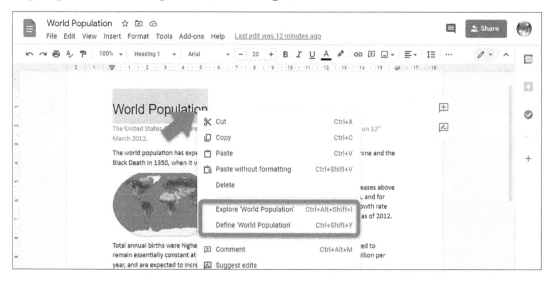

Select 'explore…' to do a Google search for the phrase, or select 'define…' to look it up in the dictionary.

Here, I've used 'lookup' to look up the word 'population'

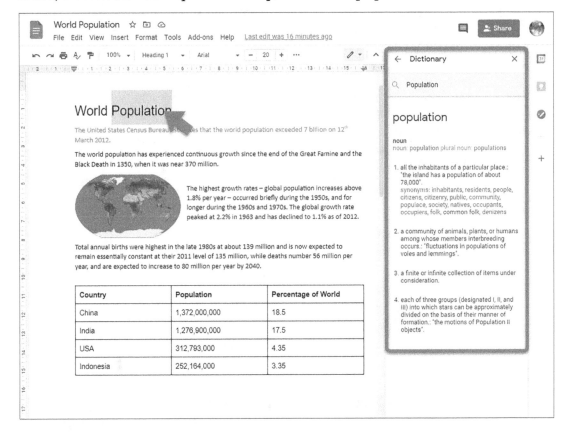

Spelling & Grammar

Google Docs automatically checks your spelling and grammar as you type. Any spelling errors are underlined in red, and grammatical errors are underlined in blue. Here, in the document below, you'll notice a couple of spelling and grammatical errors.

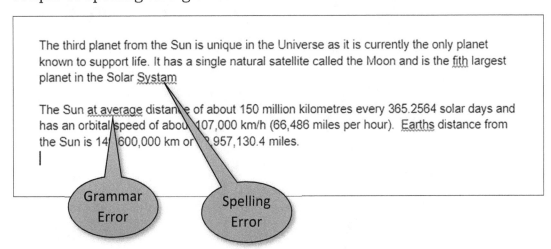

Right click on the errors to see corrections or suggestions. In the example below, click on the spelling error "systam". You'll see Google Docs spell check show you a suggestion. If the suggestion is correct, click on it to correct the error.

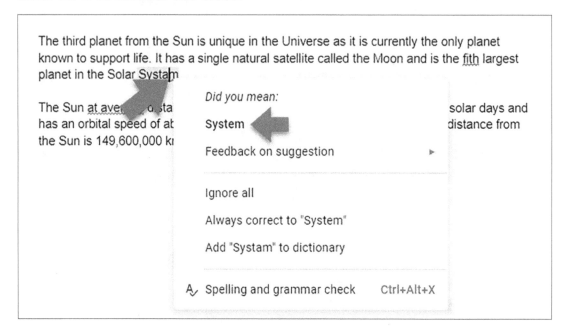

If this happens to be a common error you make with this particular spelling, select 'always correct to...'. This will automatically make the correction for you. If the error happens to be a person's name or some term you know is spelled correctly, then click 'add to dictionary'.

To run a spell & grammar check, open the 'tools' menu, select 'spelling and grammar'.

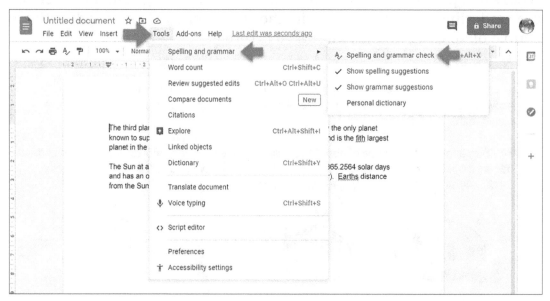

Use the left and right arrows on the top right of the 'spelling and grammar' dialog box to run through the flagged errors. Click 'accept' to correct the spelling, or 'ignore' to ignore it.

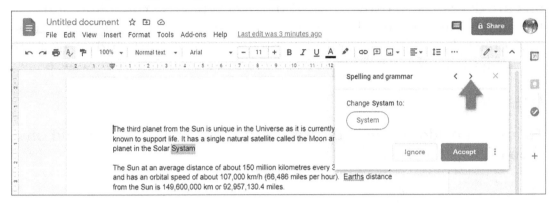

If you need to add words to your personal dictionary, open the 'tools' menu, go down to 'spelling and grammar', then select 'personal dictionary'

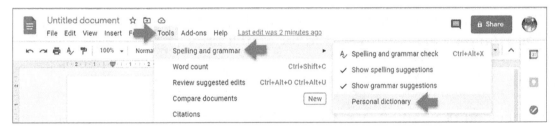

Here, you can add custom words. Type in word, click 'add'.

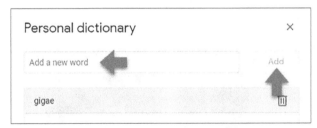

To remove a word, select the word in the list, click the trash icon.

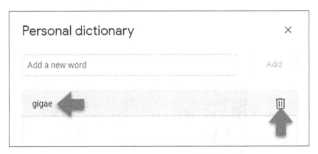

Click 'ok'.

Add-ons

You can expand Google Doc's functionality with add-ons. These add ons are developed mostly by third party developers. You'll find add-ons for adding Merge Mail, LucidChart Diagrams for creating flowcharts, and other diagrams, as well as MathType for writing and formatting mathematical equations.

Install

To install an add-on, open the 'extensions' menu, then select 'add-ons', then click 'get add-ons.

Use the search bar along the top to find an add-on you want to install. For example I'm going to search for MathType

Or click on the hamburger icon on the top left, then select a category to browse through.

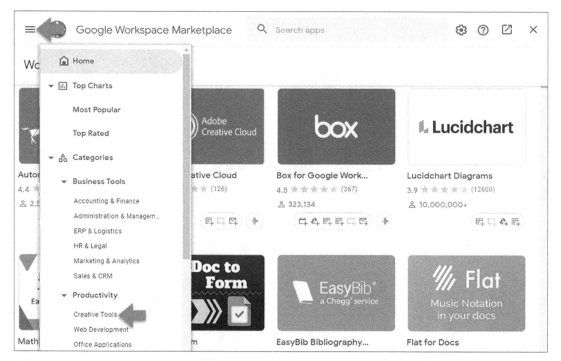

From the search results, select the add-on to install.

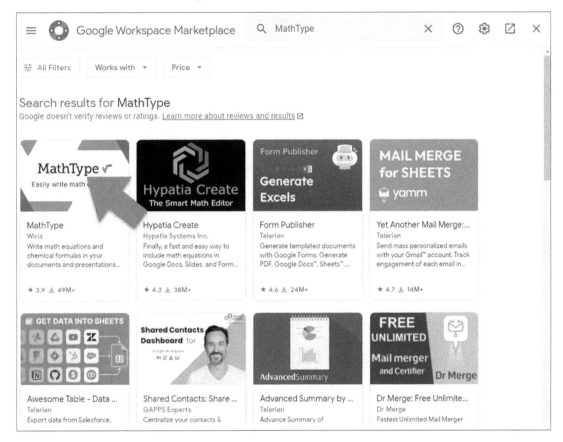

Click 'install' on the summary page. Then click 'continue' on the confirmation prompt.

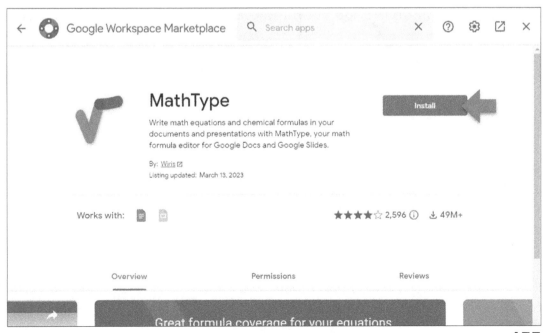

Click 'continue', choose your Google Account, then click 'allow'.

You'll find the add-on appear in the 'extensions' menu.

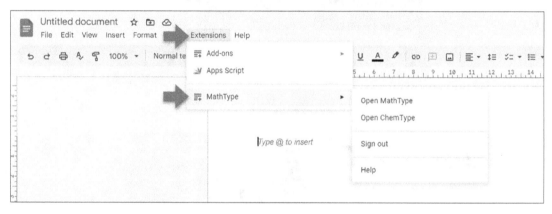

Some add-ons don't appear in the extensions menu. For example LucidChart doesn't appear. To use these types of add-ons, you'll need to open Google Drive. To do this, navigate to the following site:

```
drive.google.com
```

Click the '+' icon on the top left hand corner to create a new document.

Manage Add-ons

To manage your add-ons, open the 'extensions' menu then select 'add-ons'. From the slideout menu, select 'manage add-ons'.

Here, you'll see all the add-ons you've installed. Click the three dots icon on the top right of the addon thumbnail to uninstall.

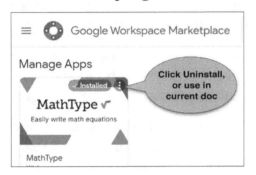

Useful Add-ons

There are many useful add-ons for Google Docs that can help enhance productivity and streamline workflow.

Grammarly is an add-on that checks your writing for grammatical errors, spelling mistakes, and style issues. It offers suggestions for corrections and can help improve the clarity and readability of your document.

DocHub is a PDF editing and signing tool that lets you annotate, highlight, and edit PDF files directly in Google Docs. It's useful for anyone who works with PDFs on a regular basis.

Coggle is an add-on that allows you to create and edit mind maps directly within Google Docs. It's a helpful tool for brainstorming and organizing ideas.

DocuSign is an add-on that allows you to sign and send documents for signature directly from Google Docs. It's useful for anyone who needs to sign and send documents quickly and securely.

Using Tablets

You can use Google Docs on a tablet or phone. You can download the app for an iPhone/iPad, or for an android phone or tablet.

In this section, we'll take a look at how to get started with Google Docs on a tablet using the app.

We'll go through downloading and installing the app on your tablet, then take a look at some basics on how to open documents, format text, add tables and images.

- Download Google Docs

- Getting Started

- Formatting Text

- Paragraph Formatting

- Insert Images

- Resize Image

- Insert Table

- Insert Row

- Insert Column

- Format your Table

Download Google Docs

To download the Google Docs app, open the Google Play Store on an android device, or the App Store on an iPhone/iPad. In this demo, I will be using an iPad.

Open the Apps Store, then search for google docs. Tap 'get' to install.

Getting Started

Once Google Docs has installed itself, you'll find the icon on your home screen. Tap on it to launch the app.

The first time you run the app, you'll need to sign in with your Google Account. To do this, tap the 'sign in' icon on the bottom left.

Enter your Google Account email address and password.

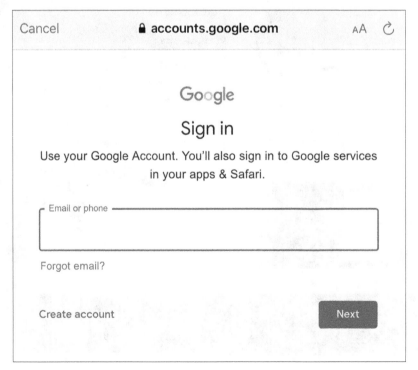

You'll land on the Google Docs home screen. Let's take a look around. Along the top you'll see an icon to open the sidebar, a search field, file selection field, and your profile icon on the right to change your Google Account Settings.

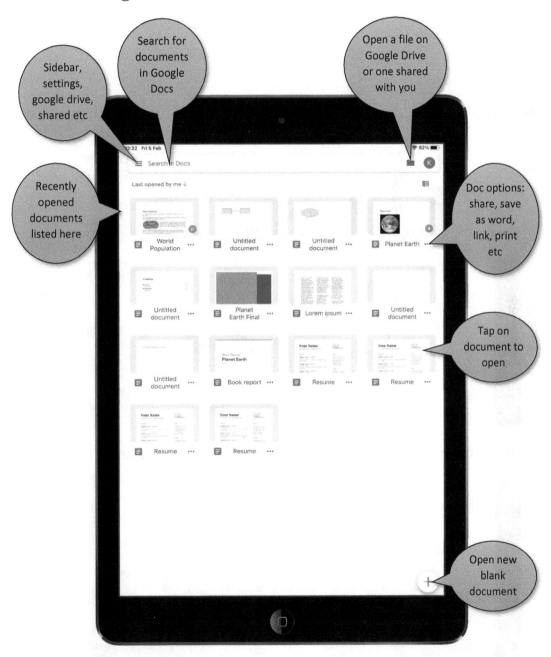

Select a document from the recently used list, or click the plus icon on the bottom right, then select 'new document' from the popup to open a blank document. In this example, I'm going to open a blank document.

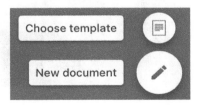

Give the document a meaningful name, then tap 'create'.

Once you've opened your document, you'll land on the editing screen.

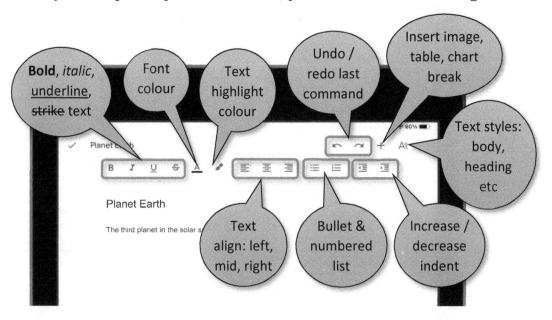

At the bottom of the screen, you'll see your on screen keyboard.

Formatting Text

To format text first open your document, then tap the 'edit' icon on the bottom right of the screen.

Next you need to select the text you want to format. To do this, double-tap on the location in the document you want to format. You'll see a blue marker appear on the text.

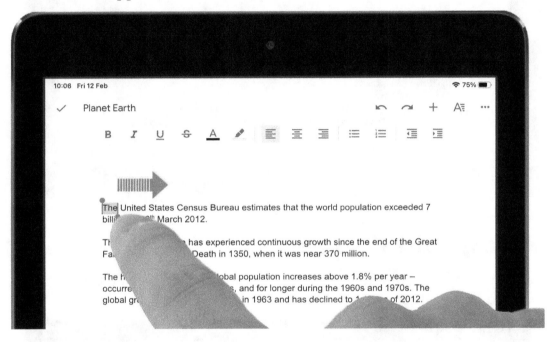

Use your finger to move the blue markers so they highlight the text you want.

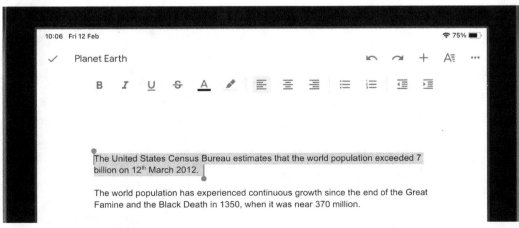

Tap the format icon on the top right. From the drop down menu select the 'text' tab. Here, you can select **bold**, *italic*, <u>underlined</u>, ~~striketext~~, superscript and subscript. Underneath you can change the text style, font typeface, font size, and text colour. Just tap on the option you want to apply to your selected text.

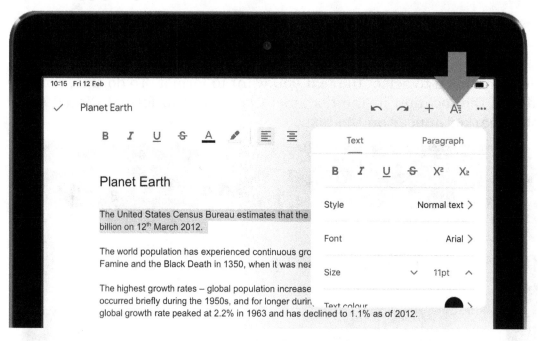

Paragraph Formatting

To align text, set indents, or adjust line spacing, select the text you want to adjust, then tap the format icon.

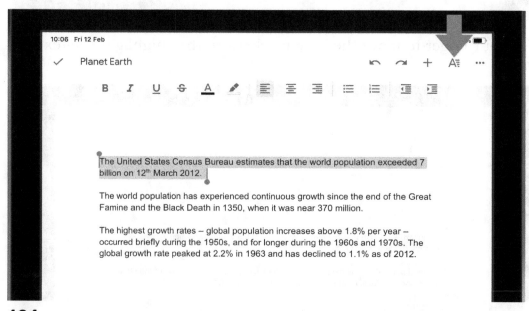

Select the 'paragraph' tab on the top of the drop down dialog box. Here, you can adjust the text alignment (left, centre, right, full). You can increase or decrease line indents, you can create numbered and non-numbered lists, and adjust the line spacing.

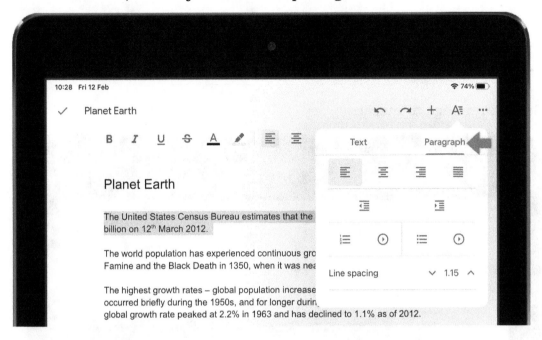

Insert Images

You can insert images saved in your photos on your tablet or directly from your camera. To do this, tap the line in your document where you want the image to appear. Tap the 'plus' icon on the top right, then select 'image' from the drop down menu.

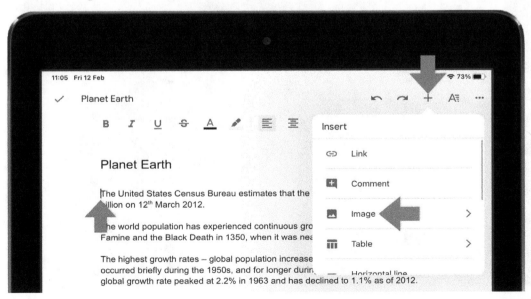

Select 'from photos' to select an image from your photo albums, or select 'from camera' to take one with your tablet's on-board camera.

Select an image to insert...

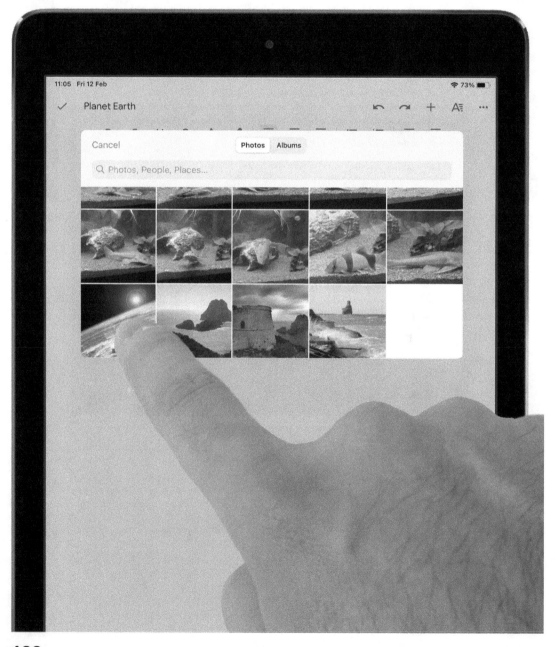

Resize Image

To resize an image, select it in your document. You'll notice a border appear around the image with resize handles appear

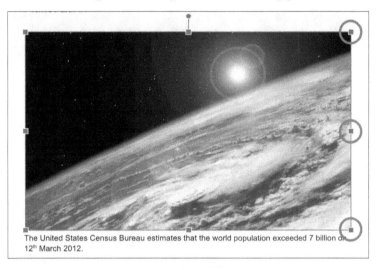

Tap and drag these handles to resize.

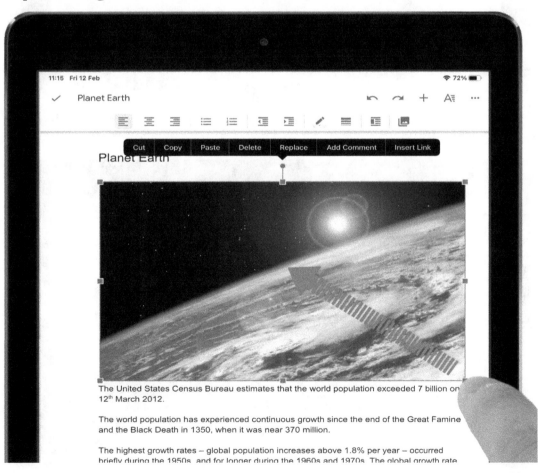

Insert Table

Tap the location in your document where you'd like the table to appear. Then tap the 'plus' icon on the top right of the screen.

Choose the number of rows and columns you want in your table, then tap 'insert table'.

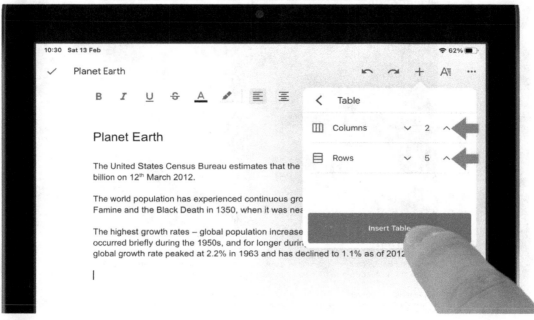

Insert Row

In our table, lets add a row between 'india' and 'USA'. To do this, tap in the row 'india' is in.

Country	Population	Percentage of World
China	1,372,000,000	18.5
India	1,276,900,000	17.5
USA	312,793,000	4.35
Indonesia	252,164,000	3.35

Tap the 'format' icon on the top right, then select the 'table' tab. Select 'row below'

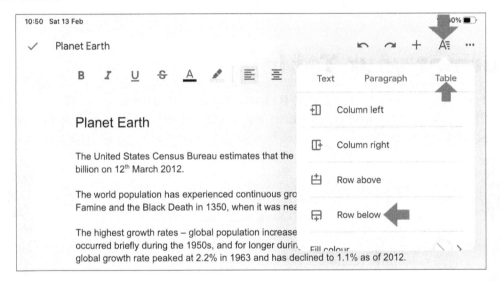

Insert Column

In our table, lets add a column between 'population' and 'percentage of world'. To do this, tap in the column 'percentage of world' is in.

Country	Population	Percentage of World
China	1,372,000,000	18.5
India	1,276,900,000	17.5
USA	312,793,000	4.35
Indonesia	252,164,000	3.35

Tap the 'format' icon on the top right, then select the 'table' tab. Select 'column left'

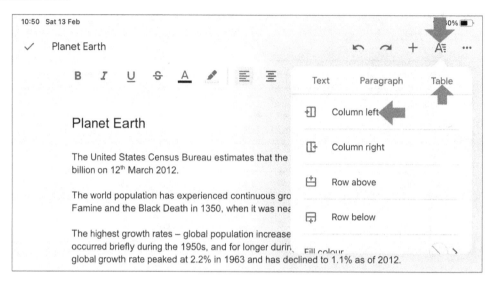

Format your Table

First select the cells you want to format. To do this tap on the first cell, you'll see a blue border appear with two dots either side. These are called resize handles.

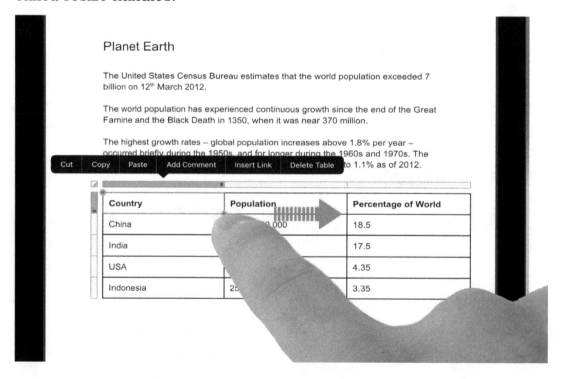

Tap and drag these handles to select the cells you want.

Tap the 'format' icon on the top right, then select the 'table' tab.

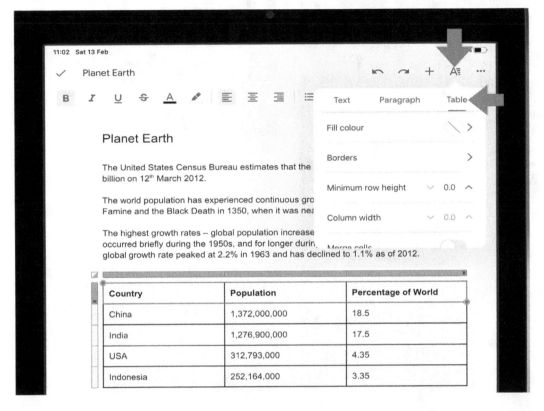

Here, you can change your fill colour, borders, row height and column width.

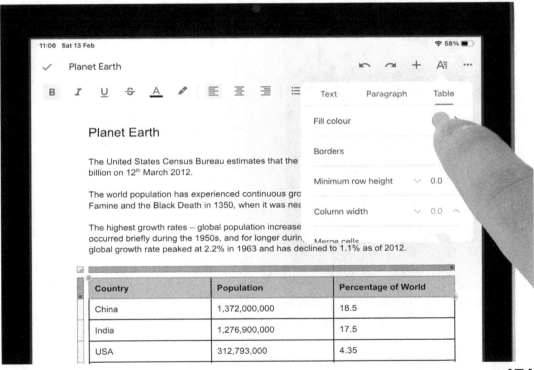

9

Using Google Drive

Google Drive is a cloud storage and synchronization service developed by Google that allows users to store files and synchronize them across multiple devices including Windows, Mac, and chromebook, as well as Android and iPad/iPhone.

You get 15 GB of space on your Drive for free but you can subscribe to various storage plans to suit your needs.

- Opening Google Drive

- On the Web

- The App

- Getting Around Google Drive

- Sync Files with your Computer

- Google Drive for Desktop

- Backup and Sync

Have a look at the video resources section. Open your web browser and navigate to the following website.

e l l u m i n e t p r e s s . c o m /
google-drive

Opening Google Drive

Once you've created your Google Account, you can access Google Drive in any web browser (ideally chrome), or from the Google Drive App if you're using a tablet or phone

On the Web

To access Google Drive on the web, open your web browser, then navigate to the following website.

`drive.google.com`

The App

If you're using Google Drive on a tablet or phone, open the app store then download Google Drive if you haven't already done so.

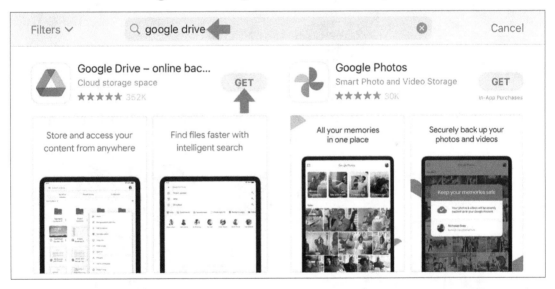

You'll find the Google Drive app on your home screen.

Just tap on the icon to start the app

Getting Around Google Drive

Once you sign into Google Drive using your web browser, you'll land on the home screen. Let's take a look. Down the left hand side panel you'll see some options.

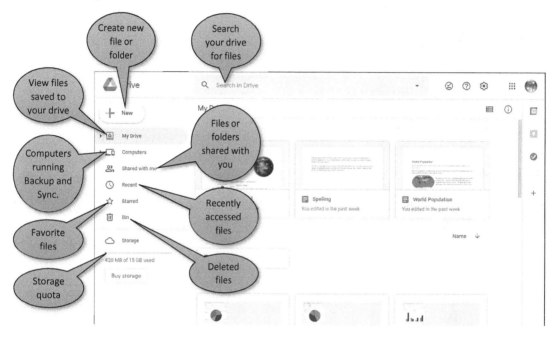

In the main screen, you'll see your 'my drive' view with a list of all the files and folders you've saved to your drive.

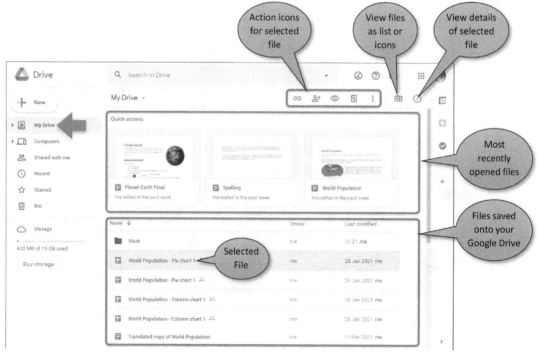

If you select a file, you'll see an icon panel appear on the top right. Here, you can create a shareable link, share the file, preview the file or delete the file.

Select the 'more options' icon and you can open the selected file with another app, add a shortcut to your drive sidebar, move the file to another folder, make the file available offline, rename the file, view the file's details, make a copy and download the file for use in another application such as Word, Excel, etc.

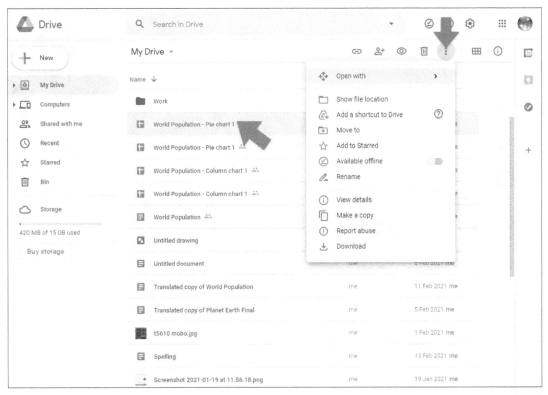

If you're using the app on your phone or tablet, things look a little different. To see all your files and folders, tap the 'files' icon on the right hand side of the icon panel along the bottom of the screen. View your files as icons as shown below - tap the 'view as' icon on the top right.

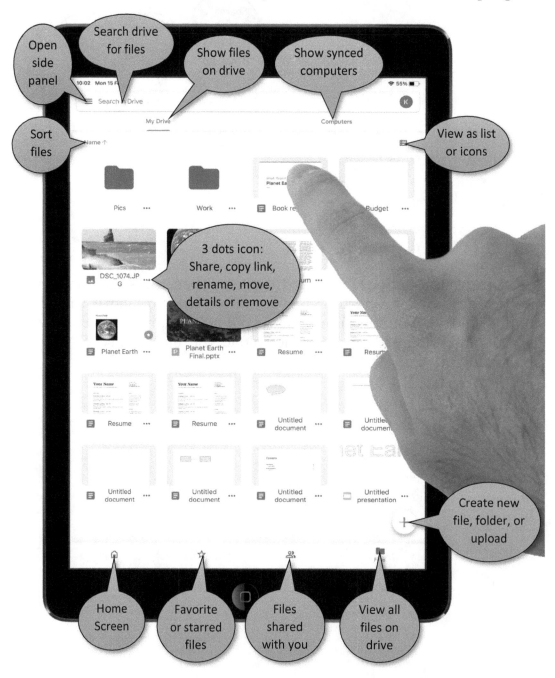

Tap on a file to open it up. Tap the three dots icon on the bottom right of each thumbnail icon to view actions you can take on that file, such as share a link, rename, view details, or delete. Tap the large plus icon on the bottom right to create a new folder or file.

Sync Files with your Computer

You can sync files with your PC, chromebook, mac, phone or tablet.

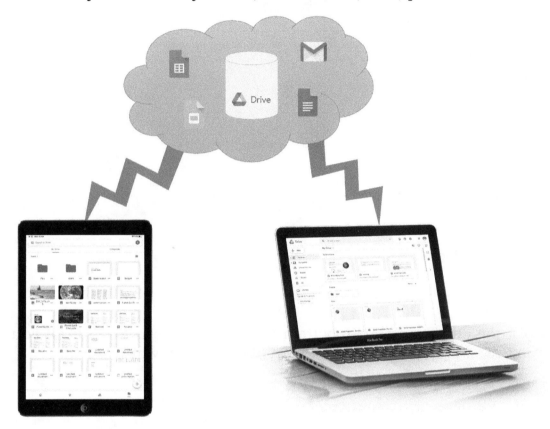

To sync files between your computers and Google Drive, you'll need to download and install the Google Drive for Desktop or Backup and Sync utility. To do this open your web browser and navigate to the following website.

```
www.google.com/drive/download
```

Google Drive for Desktop

Google Drive for desktop (formerly known as Drive File Stream) is best suited for organisations using Google Drive or Team Drive to share files amongst multiple users working in collaboration. You can't use this version with individual Google Accounts.

Backup and Sync

Backup and Sync is the consumer version of the utility and is aimed at home and individual users.

To install backup and sync, scroll down the installation web page to the 'individual' section. Click 'download'.

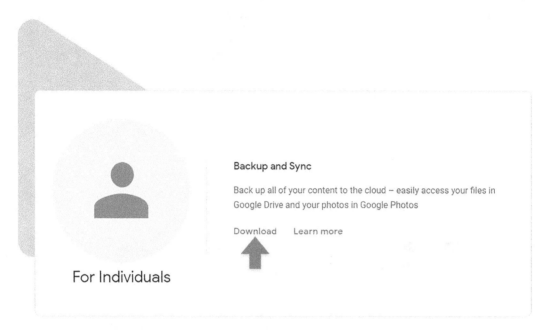

Click the download on the bottom left of your screen to begin. If you don't see a prompt, you'll find the utility in your downloads folder.

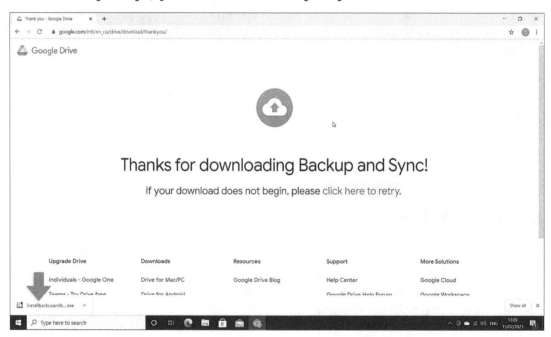

Follow the prompts on the screen to begin the setup.

The utility will download and install on your computer. After a few seconds, you'll see the install wizard appear.

Click 'get started'

Sign in with your Google Account email address and password.

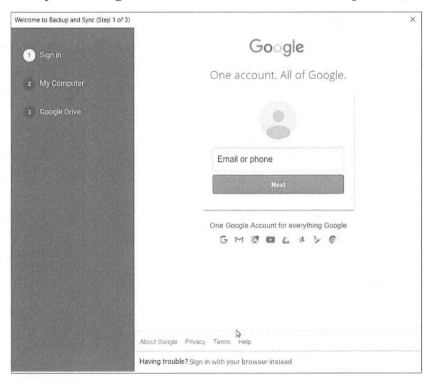

Click 'next'.

Select any folders on your computer you want to backup to Google Drive. This could be your documents folder, pictures, or any folder you save files to. These folders appear in the 'computers' section on Google Drive.

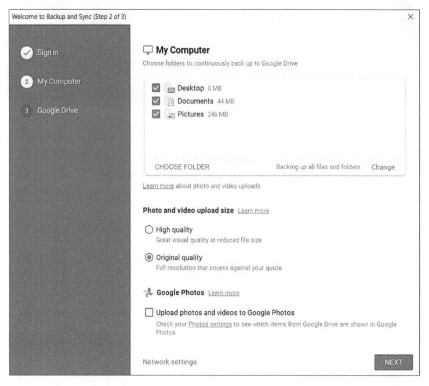

If any folders you use don't appear, click 'choose folder' then select the folder to add. You don't have to select any folders to backup and you can untick all the suggestions if you don't want to backup files. Click 'next'.

Select 'sync my drive to this computer'. Most of the time you can leave this in the default location, but if you need to change the folder or drive Google Drive syncs files to, select 'change' then choose a folder.

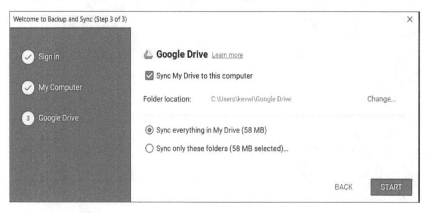

Select 'sync everything in my drive', then click 'start'.

You'll notice some icons appear on your desktop, these are shortcut icons to Google Drive, Docs, Sheets, etc.

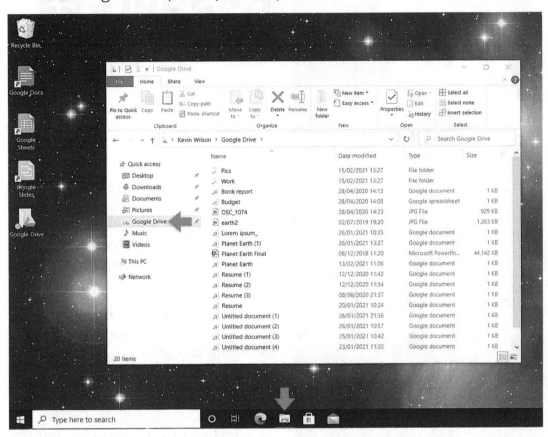

You'll also find the Google Drive folder in File Explorer. This is where you should save new files that you want to sync across to Google Drive and be available on all your devices.

You'll also see the backup and sync utility in the system area on the bottom right of the screen. Here you can view recently synced files as well as change settings.

The icons along the top of the window allow you to view Google Drive folder in File Explorer, open Google Drive in a web browser, open Google Photos.

The three dots icon on the top right, will reveal a drop down menu, where you can change settings, pause sync, or change account.

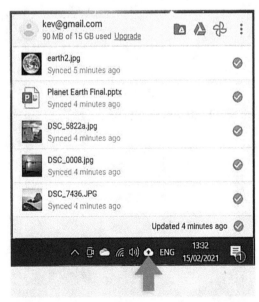

Resources

To help you understand the procedures and concepts explored in this book, we have developed some video resources and app demos for you to use, as you work through the book.

To find the resources, open your web browser and navigate to the following website

`elluminetpress.com/google-docs`

At the beginning of each chapter, you'll find a website that contains the resources for that chapter.

Video Resources

The video resources are grouped into sections for each chapter in the book. Click the thumbnail link to open the section.

When you open the link to the video resources, you'll see a thumbnail list at the bottom.

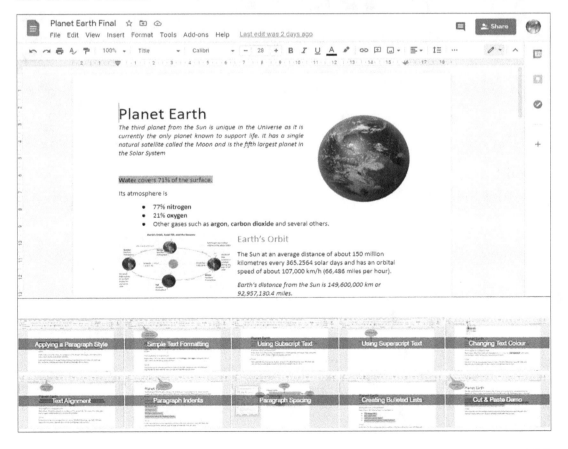

Appendix A: Resources

Click on the thumbnail for the particular video you want to watch. Most videos are between 30 and 60 seconds outlining the procedure, others are a bit longer.

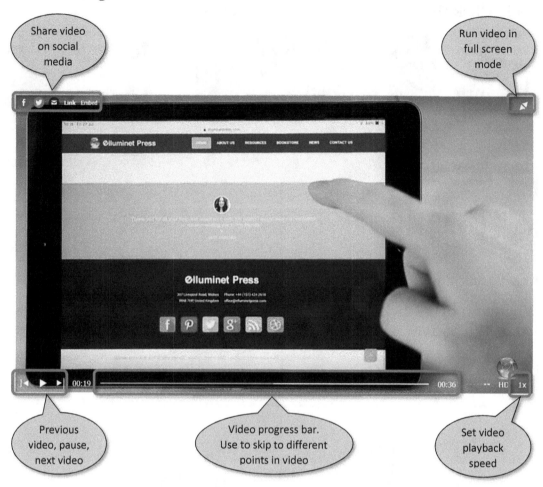

When the video is playing, hover your mouse over the video and you'll see some controls...

File Resources

To save the files into your documents folder, right click on the icons above and select 'save target as' (or 'save link as', on some browsers). In the dialog box that appears, select the 'Documents' folder, then click 'save'.

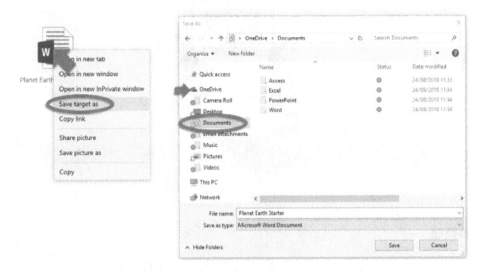

The sample images are stored in a compressed zip file. To download the zip file, right click on the zip icon on the page above, 'Sample Images. zip. Select 'save target as' (or 'save link as', on some browsers) and save it into your 'pictures' folder.

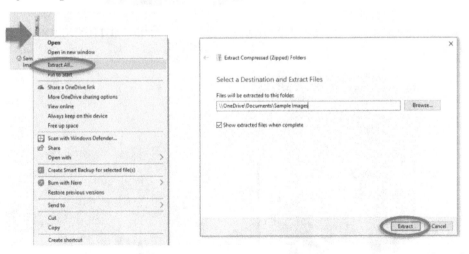

Once you have downloaded the zip file, go to your 'pictures' folder, right click on the zip file, and select 'extract all' from the menu. From the dialog box that appears click 'extract'. This will create a new folder in your pictures called 'sample images'. You'll find the images used in the examples in the books.

Scanning the Codes

At the beginning of each chapter, you'll a QR code you can scan with your phone to access additional resources, files and videos.

iPhone

To scan the code with your iPhone/iPad, open the camera app.

Frame the code in the middle of the screen. Tap on the website popup at the top.

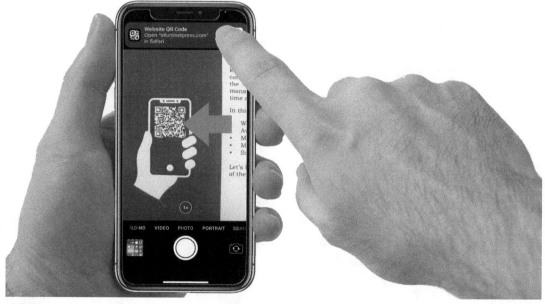

Android

To scan the code with your phone or tablet, open the camera app.

Frame the code in the middle of the screen. Tap on the website popup at the top.

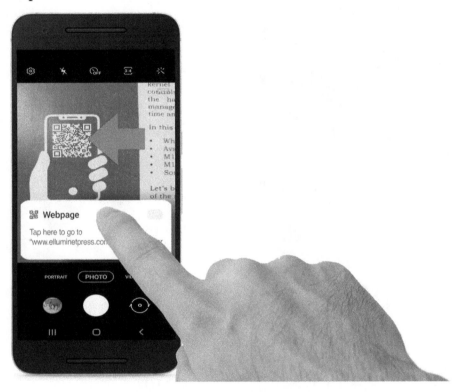

If it doesn't scan, turn on 'Scan QR codes'. To do this, tap the settings icon on the top left. Turn on 'scan QR codes'.

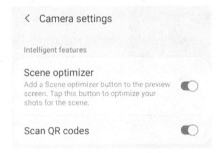

If the setting isn't there, you'll need to download a QR Code scanner. Open the Google Play Store, then search for "QR Code Scanner".

Index

A

Add Ons - 154
   Install - 154
   Manage - 157
   Useful Add-ons - 157
Align Text - 30
app - 158
Attachment - 147

B

Backup and Sync - 177
Bold - 44
Breaks - 59
Bullet List - 51

C

Case - 49
Center Align - 30
Charts - 107
   Axis Title - 111
   Background Colour - 111
   Border Colour - 111
   Customise - 109
   Data - 112
   Download & Publish - 115
   Effects - 111
   Gridlines - 114
   Horizontal Axis - 113
   Title - 111
   Vertical Axis - 113
Chrome - 22

cloud - 11
Collaboration - 116
   Accepting the Invitation to Collaborate - 119
   Chatting with Other Collaborators - 120
   Commenter - 118
   Comments - 121
     Making - 121
     Reply - 122
     Resolve - 122
   Editor - 118
   Making Edits - 120
   People without Google Accounts - 129
   Sharing a Document - 117
   Sharing a Link - 125
     Restricted Links - 127
     Sharing a Link with Anyone - 125
   Stop Sharing a File - 131
   Suggestions - 123
   Viewer - 118
Columns - 66
Contents Pages - 67
Converting Documents - 139
   ePub - 139
   HTML - 139
   Microsoft Word - 139
   PDF - 139
   RTF - 139
Copy & Paste - 41
Cropping Images - 81
Cut & Paste - 39

D
Define - 150
Dictate Text - 26
Download Chart - 115
Download Google Drive - 173
Download Google Drive App - 173
Downloading Documents - 139
   ePub - 139
   HTML - 139
   PDF - 139

Index

RTF - 139
Word - 139
Drawings - 85
Images - 90
Shapes - 87
Drive File Stream - 177

E

Email as Attachment - 147
HTML - 148
PDF - 148
Plain Text - 148
RTF - 148
Word - 148
Emojis - 69
Equations - 56
Export as Another Format - 139

F

File Stream - 177
First Line Indent - 31
Font Color - 47
Font Size - 47
Footers - 61
Footnotes - 65
Formatting Text - 163

G

Google Account - 17
Creating - 17
Google Chrome - 22
Google Docs App - 159
Google Drive - 173
Google Drive App - 173
Google Drive for Desktop - 177
Grammar - 151

H

Hanging Indent - 32
Headers - 61

Hidden Characters - 53
Highlighting Text - 46
Hyper-links - 55

I

Images - 71
   Camera on Laptop - 76
   Camera on Tablet/Phone - 77
   Cropping Images - 81
   From Google Drive - 71
   Google Photos - 72
   Insert Images on iPad - 165
   Resize Image on iPad - 167
   Resize Images - 79
   Rotate an Image - 80
   Upload from PC - 73
   Web Search - 74
   Wrap Text around Images - 83
Indenting a Line - 31
Indents - 31
   Customize indents - 34
   First Line - 31
   Hanging Indent - 31, 32
   Line Indent - 31
Inserting Footers - 62
Inserting Headers - 61
iPad - 158
iPhone - 158
Italic - 44

J

Justification - 30

L

Left Align - 30
Line Spacing - 38
Lists - 51
Lookup - 150
Lowercase - 49

M

Menus - 20
Microsoft Edge - 22

N

New Document - 25
Numbered Lists - 51

O

Opening Documents - 135

P

Padding - 99
Page Breaks - 59
Paragraph Formatting - 164
Paragraph Spacing - 37
Paste without Formatting - 43
PDF - 139
Photos - 71
Printing - 140
    Margins - 145
    Page Setup - 140
    Paper Size - 144
    Print - 143
    Quality - 146
    Scaling - 146
Publish Chart - 115

R

Resize Images - 79
Resources - 182
Right Align - 30
Rotate an Image - 80
Ruler - 34
Rulers - 21

S

Section Breaks - 59
Selecting Text - 29
Sharing - 116
Sharing a Document - 117

Sign In - 18
Smart Chips - 132
Spelling - 151
   Corrections - 152
   Suggestions - 152
Start Screen - 19
Styles - 50
Subscript - 45
Superscript - 45
Symbols - 52
Sync - 177
Sync Files with your Computer - 177

T

Tables - 93
   Borders - 97
   Cell Alignment - 100
   Cell Color - 95
   Cell Padding - 99
   Column Width - 102
   Delete Column - 106
   Delete Row - 106
   Format Table on iPad - 170
   Insert Column - 105
   Insert Column on iPad - 169
   Inserting Tables - 93
   Insert Row - 103
   Insert Row on iPad - 169
   Insert Table on iPad - 168
   Merge Cells - 101
   Row Height - 102
   Split Cells - 101
   Text Formatting - 95
Tablets - 158
Tabs - 35
Template - 25
Text Align - 30
Text Color - 47
Text Size - 47
Text Wrap - 83
Titlecase - 49

Toolbars - 20
Translation - 149

U
Underlined - 44
Uploading Documents - 137
Uppercase - 49

V
Voice Commands - 28
Voice Dictation - 26

W
WordArt - 86
Wrap Text - 83

SOMETHING
NOT COVERED?

We want to create the best possible resources to help you learn and get things done, so if we've missed anything out, then please get in touch using the links below and let us know. Thanks.

---

 office@elluminetpress.com

 elluminetpress.com/feedback

Printed in the USA
CPSIA information can be obtained
at www.ICGtesting.com
LVHW080204131023
761007LV00010B/405

9 781913 151454